Series Adviser C

Audio CD included

Navigate
Workbook with key

A2 Elementary

Contents

🔑 **Oxford 3000™** *Navigate* has been based on the Oxford 3000 to ensure that learners are only covering the most relevant vocabulary.

1 Your world — page 4
Grammar
- present simple *to be* — 5
- possessive determiners — 6
- possessive *'s* — 7

Vocabulary
- countries, nationalities and languages — 4
- family — 6
- regular and irregular plurals — 8
- vocabulary review — 8

Speaking
- asking for personal information and checking you understand — 9

Writing
- a personal profile — 9

2 My day — page 10
Grammar
- present simple and adverbs of frequency — 10
- present simple negative — 12

Vocabulary
- daily activities — 11
- telling the time — 12
- verb + preposition phrases — 14
- vocabulary review — 14

Speaking
- making suggestions and arrangements — 15

Writing
- describe where you live — 15

Listening for pleasure
- Adult education — 16

Review: Units 1 and 2 — 17

3 The world of work — page 18
Grammar
- *yes/no* questions — 19
- *Wh-* questions — 21

Vocabulary
- jobs — 18
- work — 20
- *-er* suffixes — 22
- vocabulary review — 22

Speaking
- making requests — 23

Writing
- opening and closing an email — 23

4 Places and things — page 24
Grammar
- *there is/there are* — 25
- articles *a/an*, *the*, – — 27

Vocabulary
- places in towns and cities — 24
- rooms and furniture, prepositions of place — 26
- opposite adjectives — 28
- vocabulary review — 28

Speaking
- asking for and giving directions — 29

Writing
- imperatives — 29

Reading for pleasure
- The museums of Manhattan — 30

Review: Units 3 and 4 — 31

5 Clothes and shopping — page 32
Grammar
- *can/can't/could/couldn't* — 33
- present continuous — 34
- present continuous or present simple — 35

Vocabulary
- shopping — 32
- clothes and accessories — 34
- adjectives and adverbs — 36
- vocabulary review — 36

Speaking
- in a shop — 37

Writing
- a product review — 37

6 The past — page 38
Grammar
- *was* and *were* — 38
- past simple regular verbs — 40

Vocabulary
- time expressions — 39
- common regular verb collocations — 41
- adverbs of degree — 42
- vocabulary review — 42

Speaking
- showing interest as a listener — 43

Writing
- write a tweet or a text message — 43

Listening for pleasure
- A guided tour of Stratford-upon-Avon — 44

Review: Units 5 and 6 — 45

7 Health and fitness — page 46

Grammar
- past simple irregular verbs — 47
- past simple negative — 48

Vocabulary
- a healthy lifestyle — 46
- sports and fitness — 48
- easily confused words — 50
- vocabulary review — 50

Speaking
- opinions, agreeing and disagreeing — 51

Writing
- post a website comment — 51

8 Travel and transport — page 52

Grammar
- past simple questions — 53
- have to/don't have to/should/shouldn't — 54

Vocabulary
- holidays — 52
- transport — 54
- expressions with *get*, *take* and *have* — 56
- vocabulary review — 56

Speaking
- at the train station — 57

Writing
- email: a perfect holiday — 57

Reading for pleasure
- An extract from *The Silent Brothers* — 58

Review: Units 7 and 8 — 59

9 Cooking and eating — page 60

Grammar
- countable and uncountable nouns — 60
- *much/many* and quantifiers — 62

Vocabulary
- food and drink — 60
- in the kitchen — 63
- say numbers — 64
- vocabulary review — 64

Speaking
- in a restaurant — 65

Writing
- asking about and recommending a place to eat — 65

10 The world around us — page 66

Grammar
- comparative adjectives — 67
- superlatives — 69

Vocabulary
- the weather — 66
- nature and geography — 68
- collocations — 70
- vocabulary review — 70

Speaking
- reasons and preferences — 71

Writing
- describe a place — 71

Listening for pleasure
- A TV cookery programme — 72

Review: Units 9 and 10 — 73

11 Working together — page 74

Grammar
- *going to* for plans and intentions — 75
- infinitive of purpose — 77

Vocabulary
- verb + noun collocations — 74
- technology — 76
- making adjectives stronger — 78
- vocabulary review — 78

Speaking
- offering to do something — 79

Writing
- a notice — 79

12 Culture and the arts — page 80

Grammar
- present perfect simple — 80
- present perfect simple and past simple — 83

Vocabulary
- verb and noun phrases — 81
- films — 82
- past participles — 84
- vocabulary review — 84

Speaking
- on the phone — 85

Writing
- a review — 85

Reading for pleasure
- An extract from *Les Misérables* — 86

Review: Units 11 and 12 — 87

Audioscripts — page 88

Answer key — page 96

1 Your world

1.1 Multicultural cities

Vocabulary countries, nationalities and languages

1a Look at the map. Match the numbers to the countries in the box, then write the nationality.

| Britain | China | France | Greece | Italy | Mexico |
| Pakistan | Poland | Turkey | the UAE | ~~the USA~~ | Vietnam |

1 _the USA – American_   7 _____
2 _____   8 _____
3 _____   9 _____
4 _____   10 _____
5 _____   11 _____
6 _____   12 _____

b 1.1))) Listen and check.

c 1.1))) Listen again. Pause the listening and repeat after each word. Copy the word stress.

2 Look at the countries on the map in exercise 1a. What is the main language in each country?

1 _the USA – English_   7 _____
2 _____   8 _____
3 _____   9 _____
4 _____   10 _____
5 _____   11 _____
6 _____   12 _____

PRONUNCIATION word stress

3a Put the languages from exercise 2 into the correct columns.

o	Oo	oO	Ooo	oOoo	oooO
	English				

b 1.2))) Listen and check.

c 1.2))) Listen again and repeat.

4 Complete the texts about Hong Kong, Senegal and Jamaica using words from the boxes. There is one word in each box that you do not need to use.

| ~~China~~ Chinese (x2) England English |

Hong Kong is a city in ¹ _China_ . The people from Hong Kong are ² _____ and the main languages in the city are ³ _____ and ⁴ _____ .

| Africa French Senegal Senegalese |

The main city in ⁵ _____ is Dakar and the main language in the city is ⁶ _____ . People from Senegal are ⁷ _____ .

| city country language nationality village |

Jamaica is a ⁸ _____ in the Caribbean. The main ⁹ _____ in Jamaica is Kingston, which has 600,000 people. The ¹⁰ _____ of people from Jamaica is Jamaican and their main ¹¹ _____ is Jamaican English.

4 Oxford 3000™

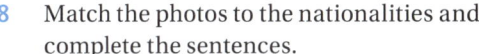

Grammar present simple *to be*

5   Make positive (+) and negative (−) sentences.
1   (−) They _aren't_ students.
2   (+) I _____ Moroccan.
3   (−) Jorge's wife _____ a teacher.
4   (+) Sara and Mahmud _____ our neighbours.
5   (−) Henry _____ happy in his job.
6   (+) The main language in Brazil _____ Portuguese.
7   (+) We _____ from Genoa, in Italy.
8   (−) You _____ in my class.

6   Make questions and short answers.
1   you / from Thailand? ✓   _Are you from Thailand? Yes, I am._
2   Mary / a student? ✗   _____
3   Lily and Sergei / married? ✓   _____
4   your house / near a supermarket? ✓   _____
5   the children / at school? ✗   _____
6   you and Tony / Irish? ✗   _____
7   Naila's husband / from Iraq? ✓   _____
8   we / late? ✓   _____
9   you / our new teacher? ✗   _____

7a Complete the conversation between Josh (J) and Amelie (A) with the questions in the list.
- Are you a teacher?
- Are you French?
- Are you married?
- Are your neighbours French-Canadian?
- ~~What's your name?~~
- What's your nationality?
- Where is your home?

J   ¹ _What's your name?_
A   Amelie.
J   That's a French name. ² _____
A   No, I'm not French.
J   ³ _____
A   I'm from Quebec, in Canada. The main language in Quebec isn't English, it's French, so I'm French-Canadian.
J   ⁴ _____
A   My home is in Montreal – it's a big city in Quebec.
J   ⁵ _____
A   No, they aren't French-Canadian. My neighbours are from the USA.
J   ⁶ _____
A   Yes, I am. My husband's a teacher at the university.
J   ⁷ _____
A   No, I'm not a teacher. I'm a doctor at the hospital.

b   1.3))) Listen and check.

8   Match the photos to the nationalities and complete the sentences.

German   Italian   Japanese   ~~Pakistani~~
South Korean   ~~Spanish~~

1   The airline _is Pakistani_.

2   The dancers _are Spanish_.

3   The video games _____.

4   The car _____.

5   The food _____.

6   The phones _____.

I can ...	Very well	Quite well	More practice
talk about countries, nationalities and languages.	○	○	○
describe people using the verb *to be*.	○	○	○

1.2 Family

Grammar possessive determiners

1a Match the words in column 1 to the words in column 2.

1 I	a your
2 you	b its
3 he	c their
4 she	d our
5 it	e my
6 we	f her
7 they	g his

b 1.4))) Cover exercise **1a**. Listen to the subject pronoun and say the possessive pronoun. Then listen and check.

2 Choose the correct options.
1 *I / My* husband and *I / my* have a new house.
2 *We / Our* office is near the train station.
3 Latif and Rana are from Turkey. *They / Their* are our neighbours.
4 **A** Excuse me, are *you / your* Samir?
   B Yes, I am. What's *you / your* name?
5 We're from a small town in Greece. *It's / Its* name is Nafplio. *It's / Its* a very nice town.
6 *She / Her* is Amy's teacher. *She / Her* husband is my doctor.
7 Gino's car is a Fiat, but *his / he's* wife has a Toyota.

3 Complete the text. Use the words in the box.

> her   his   its   my   our   their   ~~your~~

A typical family

What's a typical family in ¹ _your_ country? In the UK, a typical family is a mother, a father and two children – plus a dog or a cat! We're a typical family from a village in the west of England. There's me and ² _____ husband – ³ _____ name's David – and ⁴ _____ two children. ⁵ _____ names are Rosemary and Harry. We also have a cat – ⁶ _____ name is Ezzie. David's mum lives in the village, too – ⁷ _____ house is across the road.

Vocabulary family

4 Read about two family businesses and underline the family words.

FAMILY BUSINESSES

1 Laura Biagioni and her Italian husband, Carlo, have a fish and chip restaurant. Their daughter, Sonia, and son-in-law, Adam, work in the restaurant. Fish and chips are popular with the Biagioni family – Sonia's grandfather, Joe, was the owner of a fish and chip shop and her cousin, Andrew, and his wife, Abbie, also have a fish and chip shop.

2 All Cargo is a multinational transport company. Its main office is in Mumbai, India, but it has 200 offices in ninety countries. All Cargo is Shashi Kiran Shetty's company and it's a family company. Mr Shetty's wife, Arathi, his brother, Umesh, and his brother-in-law, Adarsh, also have jobs with All Cargo.

5a Put the family words from exercise **4** in the correct column.

Male	Female	Male or female
husband		

6 Oxford 3000™

b Add the following words to the table in exercise **5a**:

aunt child father granddaughter grandfather
grandmother grandparent grandson half-brother
mother nephew niece parent son step-father uncle

c Add other family words that you know to the table. Use your dictionary to check the spelling.

6 Read the texts in exercise **4b** again. What is the relationship between …
1 Laura and Andrew? _aunt and nephew_
2 Laura and Carlo? _____
3 Sonia and Joe? _____
4 Carlo and Andrew? _____
5 Carlo and Sonia? _____
6 Shashi and Umesh? _____
7 Arathi and Umesh? _____

Grammar possessive 's

7 Look at the 's in each sentence. Write *P* next to the sentences with a possessive 's.
1 Carlo's restaurant is in Alnwick. _P_
2 Margot's a teacher. __
3 Our daughter's name is Miriam. __
4 His wife's from Jamaica. __
5 This book's my English dictionary. __
6 The park is near my uncle's house. __
7 Where's your friend from? __
8 I'm Emily's grandmother. __

8 Look at the photo and complete the sentences about Sancho and his family.
1 Alfredo and Maria are _Sancho's_ parents.
2 Ana is Alfredo and _____ daughter-in-law.
3 Manuel is _____ brother.
4 Maria's _____ name is Sancho.
5 Isabel and Manuel's _____ name is Alfredo.
6 Manuel's _____ name is Ana.
7 Isabel and Manuel are Ana and _____ children.

PRONUNCIATION same or similar sounding words?

9a Complete the sentences. Use the words in the box.

~~are~~ he's his our 's (x2) their they're your you're

1 My wife and I _are_ from Egypt. _____ first language is Arabic.
2 Our neighbours are very nice. _____ from India. _____ names are Sanjay and Mira.
3 Jean-Paul is from France. _____ a restaurant owner. _____ wife, Annie, is a teacher.
4 Hi. _____ the new student. What's _____ name?
5 Angela _____ parents are doctors. Angela _____ a doctor, too.

b 1.5))) Listen. Pause the listening and repeat after each sentence. Pay attention to the pronunciation of the words in each of the gaps.

10a 1.6))) Listen and look at the **bold** words/phrases in each pair of sentences. Which two words/phrases do not have the same pronunciation? __
1 **They're** Greek. **Their** car is German.
2 **Henry's** at home. **Henry's** wife is at work.
3 We **are** late. **Our** train is at nine o'clock.
4 **He's** married. **His** wife's name is Eleanor.
5 **You're** late. Where's **your** homework?

b 1.6))) Listen again and repeat.

Isabel *daughter* Manuel *son*
Alfredo *grandfather* Ana *mother* Sancho *father* Maria *grandmother*

I can …	Very well	Quite well	More practice
talk about my family.	○	○	○
use possessive 's and possessive determiners.	○	○	○

1.3 Vocabulary development

Vocabulary: regular and irregular plurals

1 Write the plural form of each word.

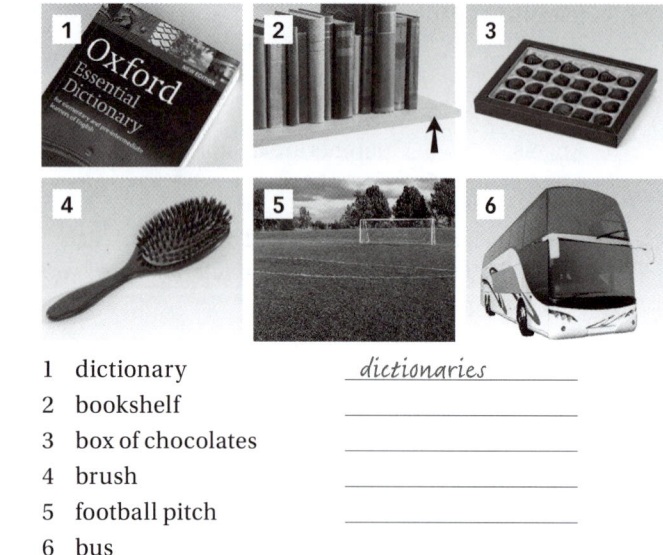

1 dictionary — *dictionaries*
2 bookshelf — _____
3 box of chocolates — _____
4 brush — _____
5 football pitch — _____
6 bus — _____

2 Complete the facts about the USA with the plural form of a verb from the box.

adult baby car child ~~city~~ class man neighbour person president road woman

FACTS ABOUT THE USA

1 Washington D.C. and New York are *cities* on the east coast of America.
2 The White House, at 1600 Pennsylvania Ave, Washington D.C. 20500, is the home of America's _____.
3 The USA has two _____ – Canada in the north and Mexico in the south.
4 Over 1 million Americans have foreign language _____.
5 There are 317 million people in the USA. 6.4% are _____ under the age of five. 13.7% are _____ aged over sixty-five.
6 Around 4 million _____ are born every year.
7 The most popular names for _____ are James and John. For _____, they are Mary and Patricia.
8 The main language is English, but 66.75% of _____ in Miami, Florida speak Spanish as their first language.
9 There are 254.4 million _____ on American _____.

Vocabulary review

3 Find the countries in the box and write them in the table. Then write a nationality and a language.

American Arabic ~~Britain~~ ~~British~~ China Chinese (x2) Emirati ~~English~~ English France French German Germany Italy Italian Mexican Mexico Pakistan Pakistani Poland Polish (x2) Spanish Turkey Turkish the UAE Urdu the USA Vietnam Vietnamese (x2)

Country	Nationality	Language
Britain	British	English

4 Complete the table.

~~father~~ granddaughter grandfather half-brother niece sister sister-in-law son step-brother uncle wife

Female	Male
mother	1 *father*
2 _____	husband
grandmother	3 _____
4 _____	grandson
daughter	5 _____
6 _____	brother
aunt	7 _____
8 _____	nephew
9 _____	brother-in-law
half-sister	10 _____
step-sister	11 _____

STUDY TIP When you learn new vocabulary, think about extra words you need to know. For example, which other countries are important to you? Find them in a dictionary and write the English name and pronunciation in your notebook.

Oxford 3000™

1.4 Speaking and writing

Speaking asking for personal information and checking you understand

1 **1.7** Listen to the conversation between a woman and the receptionist of a language college. Circle the correct answers.
   1 The woman is at the college for *a French / a Japanese / an Arabic* class.
   2 The woman's name is *Jackie / Jenny / Julie* Alamilla.
   3 The woman spells her *first name / nationality / surname*.
   4 She's *English / Irish / Australian*.
   5 She's a *receptionist / teacher / student*.
   6 Her email address is *jackie1@alamilla.com / jacqui1@alamilla.co.uk / jackie@alamilla.au*.
   7 The receptionist asks her to repeat her *name / nationality / email address*.

2a Put the words in order to make questions.
   1 's / your / What / name ?
      What's your name?
   2 your / spell / you / do / How / surname ?
      _____
   3 What / nationality / your / 's ?
      _____
   4 job / 's / What / your ?
      _____
   5 your / 's / What / address / email ?
      _____
   6 repeat / can / your / first name, / you / please / Sorry, ?
      _____

b **1.8** Listen and repeat the questions from exercise **2a**. Notice which words and parts of words are stressed.

3 Read answers a–f and match them to questions 1–6 in exercise **2a**.
   a It's Michael Hodges. _1_
   b I'm the owner of a website business. ___
   c It's mike@hodges.co.ca. ___
   d Hodges is H-O-D-G-E-S. ___
   e Yes, of course. It's Michael. ___
   f I'm Canadian. ___

Writing a personal profile

4a Correct eight mistakes with capital letters in this profile.

> My Name is maria Martinez. my Parents are Mexican, but i am american. I'm fluent in spanish and English. I live in Los angeles.

   1 *name*   5 _____
   2 _____   6 _____
   3 _____   7 _____
   4 _____   8 _____

b Put in the missing first letter of the words. Some are capital letters.

> I am a ¹__tudent at the ²__niversity of California. ³__n ⁴__ridays, I ⁵__ork at an ⁶__talian restaurant called Arrivederci.

I can …	Very well	Quite well	More practice
use regular and irregular plurals.	○	○	○
ask for personal information.	○	○	○
write a personal profile.	○	○	○

9

2 My day

2.1 A day in the life of a scientist

Grammar present simple and adverbs of frequency

1 Choose the correct form to complete the article.

A DAY IN THE LIFE OF …

Every week we **¹**(*speak*) / *speaks* to someone with an interesting job. This week it's 35-year-old Lisa Tucker, a herpetologist in Florida, USA. Herpetologists are scientists and they **²** *study* / *studies* snakes. There **³** *is* / *are* fifty different types of snakes in Florida.

Lisa and her husband, Curtis, **⁴** *live* / *lives* in a house in the Florida Everglades. A typical day for them **⁵** *start* / *starts* at 7 a.m. when Lisa **⁶** *get up* / *gets up* and **⁷** *make* / *makes* breakfast for her ten snakes. Lisa **⁸** *write* / *writes* articles for newspapers and magazines. She also **⁹** *visit* / *visits* schools with her snakes to talk to the students.

'You **¹⁰** *meet* / *meets* lots of interesting people in this job. Some people **¹¹** *think* / *thinks* my job is very unusual, but I **¹²** *love* / *loves* my life,' says Lisa. 'I **¹³** *go* / *goes* to interesting places and Curtis and I **¹⁴** *have* / *has* lots of friends.'

2 Complete the sentences with the correct form of one of the verbs in (brackets).
1 Lisa _loves_ her job as a herpetologist. (listen to / love)
2 Jacob _____ to work every day. (play / drive)
3 Yvonne _____ English in the evenings. (study / play)
4 Miyuki _____ maths at the university. (get up / teach)
5 My husband _____ in a lab. (have / work)
6 Sven _____ after work. (relax / see)
7 Sally sometimes _____ emails to her sister. (visit / write)

PRONUNCIATION third person *-(e)s*

3a 2.1))) Listen and repeat the sentences from exercise 2.

b 2.1))) Listen again and pay attention to the pronunciation of *s* at the end of each verb. Write the verbs in the correct columns.

/s/	/z/	/ɪz/
	loves	

c 2.2))) Listen, check and repeat.

4 Put the words in the right order to make sentences.
1 early / always / morning / in / Dr Abacha / the / gets / up .
   Dr Abacha always gets up early in the morning.
2 hospital / drives / to / She / the / usually .
   _____
3 works / She / weekend / the / sometimes / at .
   _____
4 has meetings / often / doctors / other / with / She .
   _____
5 7 p.m. / before / finishes / hardly ever / work / She .
   _____
6 never / goes / She / beach / the / to .
   _____
7 in / evening / the / tired / She / always / is .
   _____

10 Oxford 3000™

5 Rewrite the sentences. Replace the words in **bold** with an adverb of frequency from the box.

| always   hardly ever   ~~never~~   never   often   sometimes   usually |

1 You're **0% of the time** late for work.
   You're never late for work.
2 Manuel **75% of the time** cooks dinner for his family.
   _____
3 Nurses **0% of the time** relax at work.
   _____
4 It's **100% of the time** very hot in summer in Dubai.
   _____
5 I **80%/90% of the time** listen to music in the car.
   _____
6 Ivan **10% of the time** writes emails to his friends.
   _____
7 We **50% of the time** see seals on the beach near our house.
   _____

Vocabulary daily activities

6 Look at the illustrations. Complete the daily activities.

a   _make_   breakfast
b   _____   a shower
c   _____   to bed
d   _____   lunch
e   _____   TV
f   _____   a book
g   _____   home
h   _____   up
i   _____   music
j   _____   friends
k   _____   to work
l   _____   video games

7 Complete the text with daily activities from exercise 6. You may need to change the form.

MY TYPICAL DAY

I work in a hospital lab and my days are very busy – I ¹ _get up_ at 5.45 every morning and I ² _____ in the bathroom. Then my wife ³ _____ for me and our two kids – I usually have fruit juice and yogurt, sometimes toast. After that, I ⁴ _____ in my car – I often ⁵ _____ on the car radio because it's relaxing.

I work from 7 a.m. till 3.30 p.m. At twelve o'clock, I stop and I ⁶ _____ – a sandwich and an apple, usually. At 3.45 p.m., I ⁷ _____. On Fridays, my wife and I like to go out and we often ⁸ _____ – it's nice to see people at the end of the week, but during the week we stay at home in the evening.

After dinner, I like to relax. I often ⁹ _____ with the children on my laptop computer and my wife ¹⁰ _____ or a magazine. We sometimes ¹¹ _____ if there is an interesting programme or film. I'm usually tired at 11 p.m., so that's when I ¹² _____.

➡ **STUDY TIP** Make true sentences about your life to practise new vocabulary, e.g. *I always get up at half past seven. I never play computer games.* Write the new vocabulary and your sentences in your notebook.

I can …	Very well	Quite well	More practice
use the present simple positive to talk about my day.	○	○	○
talk about everyday actions.	○	○	○

11

2.2 Spending time

Vocabulary telling the time

1a Match the times and the clocks.
- five past eight
- five to ten
- ~~half past nine~~
- quarter past one
- quarter to eleven
- ten past six
- ten to two
- twelve o'clock
- twenty past seven
- twenty to three
- twenty-five past four
- twenty-five to five

1 _half past nine_

7 _____

2 _____

8 _____

3 _____

9 _____

4 _____

10 _____

5 _____

11 _____

6 _____

12 _____

2 Write the times.

1 _twenty to five_
2 _____
3 _____
4 _____
5 _____
6 _____
7 _____
8 _____

PRONUNCIATION saying the time

3a 2.3))) Listen to a shop assistant talk about his day. <u>Underline</u> the correct time.
1 I get up at <u>ten to</u> / ten past seven.
2 I go to work at *five past* / *twenty-five past* eight.
3 The shop opens at *quarter to nine* / *nine o'clock*.
4 I have coffee at *ten past* / *twenty past* ten.
5 I finish work at *quarter past* / *half past* four.
6 I arrive home at *half past* / *ten past* five.
7 We usually have dinner at *seven o'clock* / *half past seven*.
8 I never go to bed before *twelve o'clock* / *eleven o'clock*.

b 2.3))) Listen again. Pause the listening and repeat after each sentence.

Grammar present simple negative

4 Complete the sentences with *don't* or *doesn't*.
1 I _don't_ drive to work. I take the underground.
2 Mikki goes to classes during the week, but she _____ go to classes at weekends.
3 Paola and her husband _____ own a car. They use public transport.
4 We _____ live in a city. We live near the beach.
5 I drink coffee because I _____ like tea.
6 You always listen to Jim, but you _____ listen to me!
7 Phillip's a maths teacher, but he _____ like his job.
8 The museum opens on Saturday, but it _____ open on Sunday.

12 Oxford 3000™

5a Make negative sentences. Use the words in (brackets).

1 We work in an office. (we / factory)   *We don't work in a factory.*
2 You know Sanjay. (you / his sister)   _____
3 Bo speaks Chinese. (he / Thai)   _____
4 I have a cat. (I / dog)   _____
5 My children study science. (they / languages)   _____
6 The bus goes to York. (it / Leeds)   _____
7 Rim gets up at 7 a.m. (she / 6 a.m.)   _____
8 In the holidays we go to Mexico. (we / stay at home)   _____

6 Read the information and look at the table below. Complete the sentences about life on the RV *Atlantis*.

> Véronique Robigou is a scientist at the University of Washington. She studies volcanoes under the sea. Sometimes she does research on the RV *Atlantis*, a research boat for scientists.

	Yes	No
The boat		
1 spend a lot of time in the USA		✓
2 have six labs	✓	
The scientists		
3 cook their own meals		✓
4 have a lot of free time		✓
5 use the labs on the boat	✓	
Véronique		
6 meet scientists from other countries	✓	
7 sometimes feel seasick	✓	
8 study sea animals		✓

1 It *doesn't spend a lot of time in the USA* .
2 It _____.
3 They _____.
4 They _____.
5 They _____.
6 She _____.
7 She _____.
8 She _____.

I can …	Very well	Quite well	More practice
tell the time.	○	○	○
use the present simple negative.	○	○	○

13

2.3 Vocabulary development

Vocabulary verb + preposition phrases

1 Match 1–10 to a–j.
   1 Sam always pays
   2 My children like looking
   3 Jaime doesn't talk
   4 People usually laugh
   5 I hate listening
   6 We don't usually arrive
   7 You hardly ever ask
   8 I don't like waiting
   9 It's a good idea to think
   10 My children never agree

   a with me about their clothes.
   b about what you eat.
   c at funny films.
   d at my old school photos.
   e for help with your work.
   f for things with his credit card.
   g for the bus in winter.
   h at work before 8.30.
   i to pop music.
   j to his family every day.

2 Look at exercise 1. Write the prepositions for each of the verbs below.
   1 agree _with_
   2 arrive _____
   3 ask _____
   4 laugh _____
   5 listen _____
   6 look _____
   7 pay _____
   8 talk _____
   9 think _____
   10 wait _____

3 Complete the text with a verb + preposition from exercise 2.

Sleep problems?

When we don't get enough sleep, we feel tired during the day and we find it difficult to work or study. Sometimes we don't sleep because we go to bed and [1] _think about_ our problems. Sometimes there's another reason.

There are sleep labs where doctors study sleep problems and you can spend a night at one of the centres. What happens there? Well, you [2] _____ the centre in the evening and a nurse meets you and takes your personal details, then you [3] _____ a doctor to arrive. You [4] _____ the doctor about your health and about your sleep problems. After that, the nurse takes you to your room. People often watch TV or [5] _____ music in their room until they want to go to sleep.

When you're asleep, a computer studies how you sleep and records the information. After your night at the sleep centre, doctors [6] _____ your sleep information on the computer.

Do you have problems with your sleep? You can contact a sleep centre and [7] _____ more information. Some centres [8] _____ your time when you do a sleep study.

Vocabulary review

4 Write the phrases.

> get up   go home   go to bed   go to work/college
> have a shower   have lunch/dinner   listen to music
> make breakfast   play video games   read a book
> see friends   watch TV/a film

   1 Stop sleeping and leave your bed. _get up_
   2 Prepare a morning meal. _____
   3 Take a car or a bus, or walk to the place where you work or study. _____
   4 Eat a meal during the day/in the evening. _____
   5 Spend time with people you know and like. _____
   6 Return to the place where you live after work or some other activity. _____
   7 Something you do at the end of the day when you want to sleep. _____
   8 Look at a programme on a TV or see something at the cinema. _____
   9 A fun activity you do on a phone or computer. _____
   10 Stand under the water and wash your body. _____
   11 An activity that you can do with a CD player or an MP3 player. _____
   12 An activity you do when you study or relax. _____

5 Put the times in order from early to late.

> five past one   five to two   half past one   one o'clock
> quarter past one   quarter to two   ten past one
> ten to two   twenty past one   twenty to two
> twenty-five past one   twenty-five to two   two o'clock

   1 _one o'clock_   6 _____   11 _____
   2 _____   7 _____   12 _____
   3 _____   8 _____   13 _____
   4 _____   9 _____
   5 _____   10 _____

➡ **STUDY TIP** Look up new verbs in your dictionary and see if they go with a preposition. Write the verb and the preposition in your notebook.

2.4 Speaking and writing

Speaking — making suggestions and arrangements

1 Rearrange the words to make sentences.
1 you / out / dinner / to go / Would / like / for / tonight ?
   Would you like to go out for dinner tonight?
2 I'm / I'm / busy / sorry, / but / this evening .
   ___
3 tomorrow / you / Are / free ?
   ___
4 I'd / to / love / Yes, .
   ___
5 the / meet / at / Let's / train station .
   ___
6 that new restaurant / Do / want / you / near the park / to try ?
   ___
7 shall / meet / we / Where ?
   ___
8 nice / Yes, / sounds / that .
   ___
9 to eat / What / do you / time / want ?
   ___
10 but / plans / Thanks, / I have / I'm afraid / tonight .
   ___

2a Write the sentences from exercise **1a** under the correct heading.

Making suggestions/ arrangements	Accepting	Refusing
Would you like to go out for dinner tonight?		

b 2.4))) Listen, check and repeat the sentences. Copy the pronunciation.

3a Complete the conversation with sentences from exercise **2a**.
A ¹ *Would you like to go out for dinner tonight?*
B I'm sorry, but I'm busy this evening.
A ² ___
B Yes, I am.
A ³ ___
B Yes, I'd love to.
A ⁴ ___
B Well, I usually have dinner at around eight o'clock.
A OK, let's meet at quarter to eight. ⁵ ___
B ⁶ ___
A OK. See you tomorrow at the train station.

b 2.5))) Listen and check.

c Practise saying both parts of the conversation.

Writing — describe where you live

4 Choose the correct options to complete the text.

> I love living in Bristol ¹(*because*)/ *but* it is exciting and has many things to do. It is a big city, ² *but* / *or* I can walk to the shops ³ *and* / *but* I don't need a car. I usually go out for dinner ⁴ *or* / *because* watch a film with friends on Friday.

5 Complete the text with *and*, *but*, *or* or *because*.

> At the weekend, my husband likes getting up late, ¹_____ my favourite thing to do is to get up early and go to the beach. I like going out on our boat ²_____ it is very quiet and I can relax. I sometimes have breakfast in a beach café ³_____ read a book. Then at half past ten ⁴_____ eleven o'clock I go home.

I can ...	Very well	Quite well	More practice
use verb + preposition phrases.	○	○	○
make suggestions and arrangements.	○	○	○
use linkers in writing.	○	○	○

2.5 Listening for pleasure

Adult education

1 Match the phrases in the box to the photos. Then use them to complete the paragraph.

> ~~get a qualification~~   learn a new skill   make new friends

1 _get a qualification_

2 _____

3 _____

A lot of colleges in Ireland have courses for adults who want to learn new things. Adult learning courses are often in the evening so people who work can go to them. Some people go to ¹_____ – a piece of paper that shows how well they do something and helps them with their work. Some people want to ²_____ like dancing or how to speak a new language, and some just want to meet people and ³_____ .

2 Match the photos to the classes.

> a jewellery-making class   a language class
> an exercise class

1 _____
2 _____
3 _____

3a 2.6))) Listen to an extract from a radio phone-in programme about adult education classes in Ireland.

b Complete the introduction with the words from the box.

> ~~autumn~~   foreign   guitar   know   listeners   schools
> write

Our next topic is adult learning. It's ¹ _autumn_ now and many adult education classes are starting. Did you ²_____ that there are over 5,700 classes at ³_____ and colleges here in Ireland?

There are lots of different courses to choose from – you can learn to ⁴_____ a book, play the ⁵_____ or speak a ⁶_____ language. Today, we want you to tell other ⁷_____ about your courses.

c 2.7))) Listen and check.

4 2.7))) Look at the words from exercise 3b. Listen to the presenter's introduction again and circle the letter in each word which is not pronounced.

1 autum(n)   5 guitar
2 know   6 foreign
3 schools   7 listeners
4 write

16

Review: Units 1 and 2

Grammar

1 Correct the sentences. Add <u>one</u> of the words or letters in (brackets) in the correct place.
  1 Angela from Greece – she's Italian. (aren't / isn't)
    <u>Angela isn't from Greece – she's Italian.</u>
  2 What's your daughter name? ('s / is)
    _____
  3 First language is Turkish. (my / I)
    _____
  4 I'm in my office on Monday morning. (always / work)
    _____
  5 We drive to work because we don't have a car. (are / never)
    _____
  6 Sanjay and parents are from India. (he / his)
    _____
  7 You a student? (are / is)
    _____
  8 Dan and Emma are Jane and Simon children. (s / 's)
    _____

2 Complete the article with the present simple form of the verbs from the box. Use contractions where possible.

   close   go   have   not like   not live   phone   study   teach
   travel   ~~work~~

Nine 'til five

Fifty-five-year-old Nancy Baker is an officer worker from Kingston in Jamaica. She ¹ <u>works</u> for a computer company, but she ² _____ her job. Her favourite time of the week is five o'clock on Friday – that's when the office ³ _____ and all the workers ⁴ _____ home for the weekend.

Nancy and her husband, Jeff, ⁵ _____ two children, Adam and Amy. They ⁶ _____ with their parents. Adam ⁷ _____ Spanish at a university in Canada and Amy is a student – she ⁸ _____ in the USA. Nancy and Jeff ⁹ _____ their children every week, and Adam and Amy always ¹⁰ _____ to Jamaica in the holidays.

Vocabulary

3 Choose the correct options to complete the sentences.
  1 Matt's (American) / Australian. He's from the USA.
  2 Polish is a language and a *country* / *nationality*.
  3 Your brother is your mum's *father* / *son*.
  4 Paris and Berlin are capital *cities* / *citys*.
  5 Teresa is my step-daughter. Her mother is my *wife* / *sister-in-law*.
  6 People in Pakistan speak *Pakistani* / *Urdu*.
  7 Your cousins are your aunt and uncle's *childs* / *children*.
  8 Rim and Naila are from *the UAE* / *Greek*.

4 Match the beginnings and endings of the sentences.
  1 My daughter never agrees   a breakfast for the kids.
  2 I sometimes see   b with anything I say.
  3 You wait here   c up and go to work.
  4 My husband makes   d past five every day.
  5 There's a train to York at six   e for the bus into town.
  6 It's 6.30 a.m. Time to get   f o'clock.
  7 I sometimes think   g about work when I'm at home.
  8 The shop closes at half   h my friends after work.

Speaking

5 Complete the telephone conversation with the words from the box.

   address   let's   love   repeat   see   sorry   want   ~~would~~

   A ¹ <u>Would</u> you like to go out for lunch tomorrow?
   B I'm ² _____ , but I'm busy tomorrow. I'm free on Saturday.
   A Great. There's a good Greek restaurant in town. Do you ³ _____ to try it?
   B Yes, I'd ⁴ _____ to.
   A OK, ⁵ _____ meet at the restaurant at eight o'clock.
   B What's the ⁶ _____ of the restaurant?
   A It's called The Olive Tree and it's at 10 Tower Street.
   B Sorry, can you ⁷ _____ that?
   A The Olive Tree, 10 Tower Street.
   B OK, thanks. ⁸ _____ you on Saturday at the restaurant.

17

3 The world of work

3.1 Jobs

Vocabulary jobs

1 Look at the illustrations. Write the jobs in the grid. What is number 12?

2a 3.1))) Listen to the jobs from exercise 1 and write them in the correct column.

Stress on first syllable	Stress on second syllable
cleaner	mechanic

b 3.2))) Listen and repeat the jobs from exercise 1. Pay attention to the stress in each word.

3a Complete the job descriptions. Use the words/phrases in the box.

badly paid   computer   hands   inside   outside   ~~well paid~~

1 My job is very __well paid__ – I earn a good salary, but I work very long hours. I have my own computer company and I often have to travel.
2 Well, I work _____ . My job is in a hospital and I look after children. I sometimes work nights. It isn't an easy job, but I love it.
3 I work with my _____ . I fix people's cars for them. It's an interesting job, I love cars and I meet lots of interesting people when I'm at work.
4 I do some of my work at home, but usually I am _____ with my camera. I take photos for magazines. It's a great job.
5 I'm a student and I have an evening job – I clean offices in the city centre. I don't really like my job. It isn't interesting and I think it's _____ – I don't earn a lot of money.
6 I'm not a businesswoman, but I know a lot about business. I write articles for business magazines and for newspapers. I work with my _____ every day – it's important in my job. I use it to write my articles and to send emails.

b Match the descriptions in exercise 3a to a job from exercise 1.
1 __businesswoman__   4 _____
2 _____   5 _____
3 _____   6 _____

18   Oxford 3000™

Grammar yes/no questions

4 Complete the questions with *are*, *is*, *do* or *does*.

> **¹ _Are_ you in the wrong job?**
>
> **Ask yourself:**
> 2 _____ you bored at work?
> 3 _____ all your work days the same?
> 4 _____ your favourite time of day the time when you finish work?
>
> If the answer to these questions is yes, it's time to think about changing jobs.
>
> 5 _____ you enjoy helping people?
> 6 _____ you speak a foreign language?
> 7 _____ your friends think that you're calm and organized?
> 8 _____ a job in education interest you?
>
> If the answer to these questions is yes, it's time to think about a career in language teaching.

5 Make questions with *is/are* or *do/does*. Use the words in (brackets).
  1 You walk a lot. (you)
     Do you walk a lot?
  2 Moscow is very cold in winter. (Moscow)
     Is Moscow very cold in winter?
  3 The boss wants to speak to me. (the boss)
     _____
  4 I'm late again. (I)
     _____
  5 It rains a lot in Ireland. (it)
     _____
  6 I need to finish this work today. (I)
     _____

6 Match the questions and answers.

> ~~No, I don't.~~   No, it doesn't.   No, they don't.
> Yes, he does.   Yes, she does.   Yes, we do.

  1 Do you get up early in the morning?
     No, I don't.
  2 Does this phone have a camera?
     _____
  3 Does his daughter play a musical instrument?
     _____
  4 Do your neighbours have a dog?
     _____
  5 Do you and John read newspapers?
     _____
  6 Does her brother like being alone?
     _____

PRONUNCIATION *do* and *does*

7a 3.3))) Listen to the questions and answers from exercise **6**. Are *do* and *does* stressed in the questions or the short answers?

  b 3.3))) Listen again. Pause the listening and repeat after each question and answer.

8 Read the article about Nancy Rica Schiff and write short answers to the questions.

> **Nancy Rica Schiff: An interesting job**
>
> Nancy Rica Schiff's job isn't unusual – she's a photographer who takes lots of photos of different people, old and young. Nancy spends her time travelling around America with her camera and taking photographs of people at work. Some of her photos are in her two books: *Odd Jobs* and *Odder Jobs*. 'Odd' means unusual, and the people that Nancy photographs have very unusual jobs. They include a horse dentist and someone who turns the pages for a piano player.

  1 Does Nancy work from home?
     No, she doesn't.
  2 Is her job unusual?
     _____
  3 Does Nancy use a camera at work?
     _____
  4 Does her job include a lot of travel?
     _____
  5 Are all of her photos in her two books?
     _____
  6 Do the people in Nancy's photos have normal jobs?
     _____
  7 Do some of the people work with animals?
     _____

I can ...	Very well	Quite well	More practice
talk about jobs.	○	○	○
ask *Yes/No* questions.	○	○	○

3.2 What do you do?

Vocabulary work

1 Put the words/phrases in the correct place.

company/no company   hours   money   no job   people   ~~places~~

1 _places_ : factory, office, home, hospital
2 _____ : unemployed, retired
3 _____ : boss, manager, colleagues
4 _____ : full-time, part-time, long hours
5 _____ : salary, earn
6 _____ : work freelance, work for a company, work for a magazine

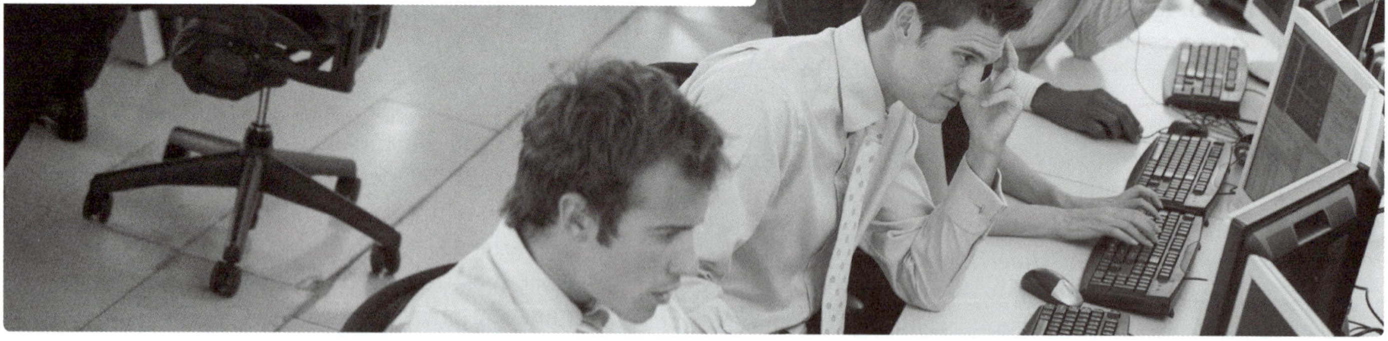

2 Complete the blogs. Use the words and phrases from exercise 1.

My name's Ada. I'm forty-five years old and I'm from Reykjavík in Iceland. I'm a software engineer – I ¹ _work for a company_ that makes software for mobile phones. I have a ² _____ job – I work thirty-eight hours a week, but I enjoy it. I earn a good ³ _____ and my ⁴ _____ are nice – we sometimes go out for meals together. I'm married to Edvard. He's a businessman. We have two children, a girl and a boy. Our son hasn't got a job – he's ⁵ _____. Our daughter is a nurse – she works in a ⁶ _____ in Reykjavík.

I'm Darren and I live in Cape Town. I'm South African. I'm the ⁷ _____ of a computer company. It's not my company – the owner, my ⁸ _____, lives in Johannesburg. I work in a big ⁹ _____ with twenty other people. It's a good job and I ¹⁰ _____ a lot of money. My dad works in a car ¹¹ _____ – the work is difficult and the hours are ¹² _____, but his salary isn't very good.

Hi. My name is Elizabeth and I live in Alice Springs in Australia with my husband, Mike. Mike doesn't work now – he's sixty-five and he's ¹³ _____. I'm a journalist. I work ¹⁴ _____ – I don't do regular hours and I don't have a boss. I write articles for the local newspaper and I sometimes ¹⁵ _____. I usually work from ¹⁶ _____ – I have an office in the house. I also have a ¹⁷ _____ job at the local college – I teach English ten hours a week there.

20   Oxford 3000™

Grammar *Wh-* questions

3 Match the question words and the answers.

1 how often — f frequency
2 what — d a thing
3 where — b a place
4 when/what time — c a time
5 who — e a person
6 why — a reason

4a Read the interview with a police officer. Complete the questions with one question word from exercise **3**. You can use the words more than once.

A ¹ _What_ do you do?
B I'm a police officer.
A ² _____ do you work?
B I work in St. Leonards Police Station in Edinburgh.
A ³ _____ do you like your job?
B It's interesting. My days are never the same.
A ⁴ _____ do you work with?
B I work with lots of different people – police officers, people in the city, school children …
A ⁵ _____ do you start work?
B Well sometimes I start at 7 a.m. and work until 5 p.m., or sometimes I work nights – that means I work from 10 p.m. until 7 a.m.
A ⁶ _____ do you have meetings?
B Oh, we have meetings every day, when we arrive at the station.
A ⁷ _____ do you do after work?
B Well, I walk a lot. I often go to Portobello Beach with my son – it's really nice there in winter and in summer.
A ⁸ _____ do you usually go to bed?
B I'm usually tired after work, so I always go to bed early.

b 3.4))) Listen and check.

5a Tick (✓) or correct the questions.
1 Where do he work?
   Where does he work?
2 When do they finish work? ✓
   _____
3 Who is you work with?
   _____
4 How often she uses English at work?
   _____
5 What time closes the shop?
   _____
6 What do usually have they for lunch?
   _____
7 Where do I go for the meeting?
   _____
8 Why does he wants to learn Chinese?
   _____
9 When you are have dinner?
   _____
10 Who lives in this house?
   _____

b 3.5))) Listen and check.

PRONUNCIATION *Wh-* questions

6a 3.5))) Listen to the questions from exercise **5a** again. Does the intonation go up or down at the end of a question?

b 3.5))) Listen again and repeat the questions. Copy the intonation.

➡ **STUDY TIP** Look up new words in your dictionary to find out how to pronounce them. A good dictionary shows you how to say a new word and which syllable(s) is/are stressed. You can hear how to pronounce a word with some online dictionaries.

I can …	Very well	Quite well	More practice
talk about work.	○	○	○
ask *Wh-* questions.	○	○	○

21

3.3 Vocabulary development

Vocabulary -er suffix

1 Make -er nouns from the verbs to name the people and things in the photos.

bake   build   compute   cook   dance   heat   paint   ~~sing~~   win

1 _singer_   2 _____   3 _____

4 _____   5 _____   6 _____

7 _____   8 _____   9 _____

Vocabulary review

2 Write the missing vowels in each job. Then translate the words into your own language.

1 b u s i n e ssm a n
2 b_s_n_ssw_m_n
3 cl__n_r
4 d_nt_st
5 h__rdr_ss_r
6 j__rn_l_st
7 m_ch_n_c
8 m_s_c__n
9 n_rs_
10 p_l_t
11 ph_t_gr_ph_r
12 ch_f
13 st_d_nt

3 Choose the correct word to complete the sentence.

badly paid   ~~computers~~   hands   inside   outside   well paid

1 Hairdressers don't work with _computers_. They usually work with their _____.
2 I sometimes work _____, but I don't enjoy it on cold days.
3 My brother works _____. He has a job in a big office in London.
4 Ping likes her job, but it is _____, and she doesn't have a lot of money.
5 Malcolm earns a lot of money. His job is _____.

4 Put the words/phrases in the correct place.

colleagues   full-time   home   long hours   a magazine   an office   a salary   ~~unemployed~~

1 be _unemployed_, be retired
2 earn money, earn _____
3 have a boss, have a manager, have _____
4 work _____, work part-time, work _____, work freelance
5 work in a factory, work in _____, work in a hospital
6 work from _____
7 work for a company, work for _____

5 Write the verb form for each of the -er nouns.

1 baker _____
2 beginner _____
3 builder _____
4 cleaner _____
5 cooker _____
6 dancer _____
7 driver _____
8 farmer _____
9 heater _____
10 maker _____
11 manager _____
12 painter _____
13 DVD/MP3 player _____
14 runner _____
15 singer _____
16 teacher _____
17 winner _____
18 worker _____

3.4 Speaking and writing

Speaking making requests

1a Make requests with *can/could* for each situation.
1 You and your wife are at the cinema – you want two tickets to see *Batman*.
   Could we _have two tickets to see Batman, please_ ?
2 You're in your English class – you want your teacher to spell 'author'.
   Could you _____?
3 You're at the library – you want to join.
   Can I _____?
4 You are at work – you want to use your colleague's pencil.
   Can I _____?
5 You and your family are in a new town – you want someone to tell you where the station is.
   Could you _____?
6 You're in a restaurant – you want to pay for your meal with your credit card.
   Could I _____?

b 3.6))) Listen, check and repeat. Copy the intonation.

2a Look at the responses to requests. Are they positive (P) or negative (N)?
1 Yes, of course. _P_   4 Sure. __
2 I'm afraid not. __   5 Yes, that's fine. __
3 No, I'm sorry, but … __

b 3.7))) Listen and repeat the responses. Copy the intonation.

3a Read the requests. Where are the people?

| at home   at work   in a café/restaurant   in a car park |
| in a school   in a shop |

1 Excuse me, could I start work a little late tomorrow?
   at work
2 Pete, can you lend me 50 euros? I want to buy this book.
   _____
3 Dad, can I borrow your phone?
   _____
4 Excuse me. Can I leave my car here?
   _____

5 Excuse me, can you help me with this exercise, please?
   _____
6 Can we have two, please?
   _____

b Match the responses (a–f) to the requests (1–6) in exercise 3a.
a Of course! What's the problem? _5_
b Yes, that's fine. It's on the table. __
c I'm sorry, that isn't possible, Tom. There's an important meeting in the morning. __
d Sure. Here you are. __
e I'm afraid not. This car park is for company staff only. __
f Yes, of course. Anything to eat? __

c Practise saying both parts of the conversation.

Writing opening and closing an email

4 Complete the two emails using the correct word in each pair.
1 Dear / Hello
2 Can we / Can I
3 See you / I'm free
4 Best wishes / love
5 Dear / Hi
6 Could you let me know / How are you
7 Can I / Could you
8 Love / Yours sincerely

⊠
¹ _Dear_____ Marion,

Thank you for your email. ² _____ meet on Tuesday?
³ _____ in the afternoon.
⁴ _____,
Paul

⊠
⁵ _____ Sarah

⁶ _____? I have a quick question. I'm in London for a meeting on Tuesday afternoon. ⁷ _____ stay at your house?

⁸ _____ Marion

I can …	Very well	Quite well	More practice
use *-er* suffixes.	○	○	○
make requests.	○	○	○
write an email.	○	○	○

23

4 Places and things

4.1 Underground towns

Vocabulary places in towns and cities

1 Replace the phrases in **bold** with a word from the box.

| a cinema   a hospital   a library   the museum |
| a railway station   the roads   ~~school~~   shops |
| swimming pool   the tourist information centre |

1 _school_   6 _____
2 _____   7 _____
3 _____   8 _____
4 _____   9 _____
5 _____   10 _____

2 Look at the map of Lightning Ridge. Name the places.

a _theatre_   f _____
b _____   g _____
c _____   h _____
d _____   i _____
e _____

PRONUNCIATION word stress

3a 4.1))) Listen to the words from exercise 2. Which syllable is stressed in each word? Write the words in the correct column.

Stress on first syllable	Stress on second syllable
theatre	

b 4.2))) Listen and repeat the words. Copy the stress.

LIGHTNING RIDGE
POPULATION 4,500

The Australian town of Lightning Ridge is 1,200 km away from the underground town of Coober Pedy. It is also an opal mining town. Four thousand five hundred people live in the town – 400 of them are students at Lightning Ridge Central [1] **place for children to learn**.

Lightning Ridge is a great place to live. It has everything you need. There's [2] **a place with doctors and nurses** and there are good [3] **places to buy things**, including a chemist and a hairdresser's. There are also nice restaurants and [4] **a place to borrow books**. There isn't [5] **a place to watch films**, but the town has a theatre and a great [6] **place to do sport in water**.

There isn't [7] **a place for trains to arrive and leave** near Lightning Ridge, but there's an airport and [8] **the things for cars and buses to drive on** are good. A lot of people visit the town and one place they visit is [9] **the place for visitors to get a town map**. Tourists usually want to see the opal mines and [10] **the place to learn about the history of the town**.

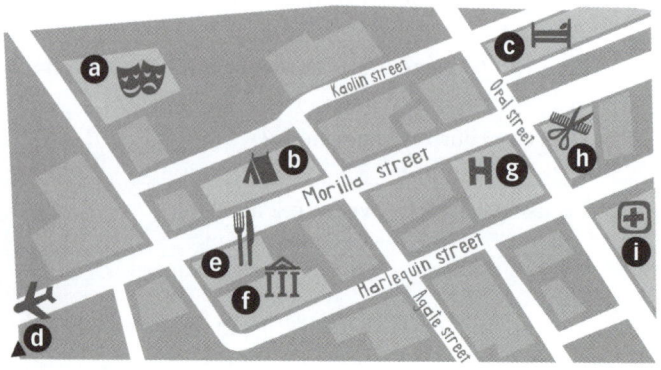

---

24 | Oxford 3000™

Grammar *there is/there are*

4 Match the beginnings and endings of the sentences.
1 There are — a night market in Hong Kong.
2 There's an — b 91 universities in England.
3 There's a   c cities in Scotland.
4 There   d 12 countries in South America.
5 There are seven e are 1,250 million people in India.
6 There are   f underground town in Australia.

5 Belchite is a small village in the north of Spain. Look at the information about the village and make sentences using *there is/there are*.

❶	a railway station	✗
❷	a museum	✓
❸	restaurants	✓ (three)
❹	a supermarket	✓
❺	any big hotels	✗
❻	a hospital	✗
❼	old buildings	✓
❽	many people	✗
❾	a tourist information centre	✓

1 *There isn't a railway station.*
2 ___
3 ___
4 ___
5 ___
6 ___
7 ___
8 ___
9 ___

6a Circle the correct form to complete the conversations.

1 A Excuse me. *Is there* / *There's* a tourist information centre in the town?
   B Yes, *there is* / *there's*. It's just near the railway station.
2 A *Is there* / *Are there* a cinema in the town centre?
   B No, I'm sorry, *there isn't* / *there aren't*. But there's a theatre.
3 A *Are there* / *Is there* any nice restaurants near here?
   B Yes, *there are* / *there're*. There's the Lanterna Restaurant in Queen Street and Nico's in Westgate.
4 A *Is there* / *Is there* a campsite near the beach?
   B Yes, *there is* / *there's*. The Sunny Days Campsite is near the beach.
5 A Are there *a* / *any* bookshops in the village?
   B No, I'm afraid *there aren't* / *there are no*.
6 A Are there many *thing* / *things* to see in the town?
   B Yes, *are there* / *there are*. There are lots of things to see and do here.

b 4.3))) Listen and check.

➔ **STUDY TIP** When you learn new grammar, write an example sentence in English and translate it into your language. Look for things that are the same and things that are different. For example, do the sentences have the same number of words? Are the words (subject, noun, verb) in the same order?

I can ...	Very well	Quite well	More practice
talk about places in towns and cities.	○	○	○
use *there is/there are*.	○	○	○

4.2 Where I live

Vocabulary rooms and furniture, prepositions of place

1a Label the diagrams using words from the box.

> a bathroom   a bedroom   a dining room   a flat   a garage
> a house   a kitchen   a living room   an office   a toilet

1 _a house_
2 _____
3 _____
4 _____
5 _____
6 _____
7 _____
8 _____
9 _____
10 _____

b 4.4))) Listen, check and repeat.

2 Complete the sentences with one of the words in (brackets).
1 The children are asleep in their _beds_ . (beds / carpets)
2 The _____ in the kitchen is old. We need a new one. (toilet / cooker)
3 Put the food in the _____ . (fridge / washing machine)
4 The _____ in the bedroom is blue. (carpet / dishwasher)
5 Your dinner is on the _____ in the dining room. (cooker / table)
6 We don't have a _____ – we take our clothes to the launderette. (dishwasher / washing machine)
7 A Where's the French dictionary?
   B It's on the _____ in my office. (sink / shelf)
8 They don't have a dishwasher. They wash the dishes in the kitchen _____ . (sink / shower)
9 In the evening, John likes to sit in the big _____ in the living room and watch television. (desk / armchair)

3 Complete the prepositions.

1 b_ehind_____
2 o_____
3 n_____ t_____
4 a_____
5 i_____ f_____ o_____
6 b_____
7 u_____
8 o_____

4 Choose the correct preposition to complete the text.

A houseboat in Amsterdam

Our home isn't a typical house. We live ¹*on*/ *above* a boat – it's one of 2,500 houseboats in Amsterdam. It has a small kitchen, a living room, a bathroom and a bedroom. We sleep in the bedroom and we have a place ² *in* / *under* the bed for our clothes. There's a window ³ *behind* / *under* the bed so we can look out at the river. The bathroom is ⁴ *between* / *in* the bedroom and the living room. It has a toilet and there's a small shower ⁵ *above* / *in* the toilet. There's a table and two armchairs in the living room, and a small TV ⁶ *on* / *above* a shelf. ⁷ *In front of* / *On* the table there's a blue carpet. ⁸ *Next to* / *On* the living room is the kitchen. We have a cooker and ⁹ *under* / *opposite* the cooker there is a sink.

Oxford 3000™

Grammar articles *a/an, the, –*

5 Rewrite the sentences with *a* or *an*.
1 Mumbai is interesting city to visit.
   Mumbai is an interesting city to visit.
2 Is there elevator in your building?
3 My parents have house near the beach.
4 I have big sofa in my living room.
5 You can visit opal mine in Australia.
6 Is there metro station near here?
7 There isn't airport in my town.
8 There's park in the town centre.

6 Read the sentences. Cross out one *the* in each sentence.
1 The Nile River is in ~~the~~ Africa.
2 There are lots of the flats in the building.
3 The capital of Thailand is the Bangkok.
4 The Prado Museum is in the centre of the Madrid.
5 We go to the cinema on the Saturdays.

7 Complete the web page about Amsterdam. Write *a*, *an*, *the* or (-) in the gaps.

PRONUNCIATION the schwa /ə/ sound

8a 4.5))) Listen to the sentences/questions. Underline the schwa /ə/ sounds.
1 My house is next <u>to</u> the park.
2 There's a supermarket opposite the cinema.
3 Do you have a map of the city?
4 Is there an airport near your town?
5 The students are in a classroom on the second floor.

b 4.5))) Listen again and write the stressed words.
1 *house, next, park*
2 _____
3 _____
4 _____
5 _____

c 4.5))) Listen again. Pause the listening and repeat after each sentence.

WHAT TO DO IN AMSTERDAM

Amsterdam, the capital city of ¹ _the_ Netherlands, is ² _____ great place to spend time. It's easy to travel to ³ _____ city because it has ⁴ _____ big railway station and ⁵ _____ airport – and it isn't difficult to find ⁶ _____ hotel.

There's a lot to see and do here. There are ⁷ _____ shops for people who enjoy shopping and ⁸ _____ restaurants with typical Dutch food, like *stamppot* or *poffertjes*. Or you can go to one of ⁹ _____ museums, such as ¹⁰ _____ Van Gogh Museum. The best way to travel around ¹¹ _____ Amsterdam is on a bike – there are 747,000 people here and over 600,000 bikes!

After a busy day, a lot of ¹² _____ visitors like to relax on ¹³ _____ boat tour of ¹⁴ _____ city at night or they enjoy ¹⁵ _____ cup of coffee at one of Amsterdam's many *koffiehuizen* (coffee houses).

I can ...	Very well	Quite well	More practice
talk about rooms and furniture.	○	○	○
use prepositions of place.	○	○	○
use articles.	○	○	○

27

4.3 Vocabulary development

Vocabulary opposite adjectives

1 Circle the correct description.

1 clean shoes / dirty shoes
2 a noisy child / a quiet child
3 a heavy box / a light box
4 a tidy desk / a messy desk
5 a big dog / a small dog
6 a new car / an old car

2 Choose the correct adjective to complete the sentences.
1 Mandy, put those *dirty* / *clean* clothes in the washing machine!
2 A Your baby is *beautiful* / *ugly*.
   B Thank you.
3 The journey from the north to the south of Africa is very *long* / *short*.
4 A Did you enjoy the play?
   B Yes, the actors were *terrible* / *fantastic*!
5 We can't go to the beach if the weather is *bad* / *good*.
6 My mother is very *old-fashioned* / *modern*. She doesn't use a computer.
7 A Can you do this exercise?
   B No, it's *easy* / *difficult*.

Vocabulary review

3 Use a dictionary to translate the places into your language.
1 airport _____
2 campsite _____
3 chemist _____
4 cinema _____
5 hairdresser's _____
6 hospital _____
7 hotel _____
8 library _____
9 museum _____
10 railway station _____
11 restaurant _____
12 road _____
13 shop _____
14 swimming pool _____
15 theatre _____
16 tourist information centre _____

4 Write the words in the correct column.

<del>armchair</del> bathroom   bed   bedroom
carpet   cooker   dining room
dishwasher   flat   fridge   garage   house
kitchen   living room   office   shelf   sink
table   toilet   washing machine

Places to live	Places in the home	Furniture
		armchair

5 Write the opposite adjectives. Choose the words from the box.

cheap   dirty   easy   fantastic   good
light   modern   new   noisy   short
small   <del>tidy</del>   ugly

1 messy — tidy
2 clean — _____
3 long — _____
4 expensive — _____
5 quiet — _____
6 difficult — _____
7 bad — _____
8 beautiful — _____
9 old — _____
10 heavy — _____
11 big — _____
12 terrible — _____
13 old-fashioned — _____

➡ **STUDY TIP** When you learn a new adjective, look it up in a good dictionary to see if it has an opposite. Write both words in your notebook and learn them together.

4.4 Speaking and writing

Speaking asking for and giving directions

1a Complete the directions. Use the words in the box.

corner end first left past straight take turn

1 on the _left_
2 at the _____ of the road
3 take the _____ left
4 on the _____
5 _____ right
6 go _____ on
7 _____ the second left
8 go _____ the cinema

b 4.6))) Listen and repeat the phrases.

2a Find the tourist information centre on the map of Lightning Ridge. Read the conversations at the tourist information centre and follow the directions on the map. Complete each conversation with a place from the box.

an art gallery the caravan park a hairdresser's the hospital the Opal Centre the school the theatre

1 **A** Excuse me, how do we get to _____?
   B Go out of the main door and turn right. Go straight on, past the theatre. It's on the left.
2 **A** Excuse me, could you give us some directions, please?
   B Yes, of course. How can I help you?
   A Thanks. We want to get to _____.
   B OK, well go out of the tourist information centre and turn right. Take the second road on the right. Turn left at the end of the road into Harlequin Street. Go straight ahead for ten minutes. Take the third turning on the right. It's on Opal Street on the left.
3 **A** Excuse me, where's _____?
   B Go out of the main door and turn right. Take the first road on the left, then turn right into Kaolin Street. Go straight on for ten minutes. It's on the corner of Kaolin Street and Opal Street.

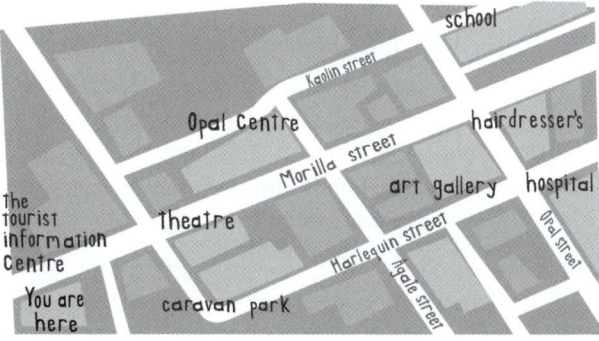

b 4.7))) Listen and check.

Writing imperatives

3 Complete the house rules with the verbs in the box.

clean don't forget don't leave don't use take wash

House rules

1 _____ the washing machine after 9 p.m. It's very noisy!

Please 2 _____ your dishes.
3 _____ your dirty cups and plates in the sink. There is no dishwasher!

Please 4 _____ the shower after you use it and 5 _____ your clothes to your bedroom.

6 _____ five other people live here!

Thanks,

John

I can ...	Very well	Quite well	More practice
use opposite adjectives.	○	○	○
ask for and give directions.	○	○	○
use the imperative to give instructions.	○	○	○

4.5 Reading for pleasure

The museums of Manhattan

1 Match the words in the box to the photos. Check any new words in your dictionary.

> ~~an artist~~   an exhibition   a painting   a statue   a theatre

1 _an artist_   2 _____   3 _____   4 _____   5 _____

2 Read the extract from the *Factfiles: New York*. It describes five museums and art galleries in Manhattan, an area of New York.

There are more than sixty museums in Manhattan. Some stay open late one or two evenings in the week, and some are free.
   The Metropolitan Museum of Art – '5,000 years of art' – is New York's biggest museum, and is on Fifth Avenue. It has three floors with thousands of paintings, statues and other things. Titian, El Greco, Monet, Cezanne, and Rousseau are just some of the names in the Metropolitan Museum. There is a garden of statues, too.
   Perhaps you are interested in American artists. At the Whitney Museum of American Art at 945 Madison Avenue you can see pictures by Edward Hopper, Georgia O'Keeffe, Jasper Johns, Willem de Kooning and many more American artists.
   The Museum of Modern Art (MoMA) is at 11 West 53rd Street. It has the world's biggest collection of modern art. There are six floors of pictures, photographs and statues. Two of the most famous pictures are Monet's *Water Lilies* and Picasso's *Les Demoiselles d'Avignon*.
   The Museum of the City of New York on Fifth Avenue, at 103rd Street, tells the story of New York from its beginning. Watch the *Timescapes* movie, and visit the exhibition *Perform* about the New York theatre.
   The Guggenheim Museum is also on Fifth Avenue, at 88th Street. The museum opened in 1959. You can see the work of Picasso, Kandinsky, Modigliani and other modern artists in this strange but wonderful museum.

Text extract from *Oxford Bookworms Factfiles: New York*.

3 Complete the notes with the answers from the box.

> ~~modern art~~   Museum of Modern Art
> Museum of the City of New York   statues   the USA

1 You can see _modern art_ at the Guggenheim Museum.
2 The Metropolitan Museum has thousands of paintings and there are _____ outside in the museum garden.
3 Go to the _____ to learn about New York from the past to the present.
4 One of Monet's most famous paintings is at the _____.
5 The Whitney Museum is a good place to see pictures by artists from _____.

4 Answer the questions.
1 Which Manhattan museum would you like to visit?
_____
_____
_____

2 What famous museums and art galleries are there in your country?
_____
_____
_____

3 What sort of things can you see in them?
_____
_____
_____

Review: Units 3 and 4

Grammar

1 Match questions (1–8) to answers (a–h).
   1 Am I late? _e_
   2 Do your parents travel a lot? ___
   3 What does Les do? ___
   4 Where's the tourist information centre? ___
   5 Is there a supermarket near here? ___
   6 Does Kerry like her job at the hospital? ___
   7 Who usually takes your children to school? ___
   8 When does the library open? ___

   a No, they don't.
   b Yes, there is. It's on High Road.
   c My husband.
   d It's next to the railway station.
   e No, you aren't.
   f Yes, she does. She loves it.
   g At half past nine.
   h He's a car mechanic.

2 (Circle) the correct words to complete the text.

Where I live

It's difficult for young people to buy ¹(a)/ *an* house in ² *the* / - south of England because houses are very expensive. We're very lucky because we have ³ *the* / *an* old house in ⁴ *the* / *a* centre of ⁵ *a* / - nice village, but the average price of ⁶ - / *a* small house in our village is £250,000.

The village is small – ⁷ *there are* / *there is* one or two small shops, but ⁸ *there aren't* / *there are* any restaurants and ⁹ *there aren't* / *there isn't* a railway station here. Fortunately, we are near a big town called Basingstoke. Basingstoke has a shopping centre with lots of ¹⁰ *the* / - shops and restaurants. Opposite the shopping centre ¹¹ *there's* / *there are* a railway station with fast trains to ¹² *the* / - London.

Vocabulary

3 Complete the words in the text.

My name's Javier and I live in Spain with my wife, Maria. I'm a ¹ busi_nessman_ and I work for a car ² comp_____ in Barcelona. It's a ³ full-t_____ job – I work forty hours a week and I travel a lot, but I like it. The job is ⁴ well-p_____ and my ⁵ collea_____ are very friendly. We work in an ⁶ off_____ near the centre of the city and we often go out together after work. Maria is a doctor at the ⁷ hosp_____. She works long hours, but she earns a good ⁸ sal_____ and she loves her work.

4 (Circle) the word that matches the definition.
   1 It's a place where people make things, e.g. cars.
      (a factory) / a manager / freelance / an office
   2 It's a great place for people who like books.
      a road / a theatre / a library / a hotel
   3 It's the room where people cook.
      a bathroom / a toilet / a garage / a kitchen
   4 It's the opposite of *on*.
      between / under / next to / behind
   5 It's something you often see in the bathroom.
      a cooker / a dishwasher / a shower / a desk

Speaking

5 Complete the conversations with the phrases from the box.

   at the end of   can you   could I   ~~get to~~   go past   near here
   that's fine   the right   turn right   where's

   1 A Excuse me, how do I _get to_ the tourist information centre?
      B Go straight on – it's ¹_____ the road.
   2 A ²_____ have a day off on Friday, please?
      B ³_____. Let me make a note in my diary to remind me.
   3 A Excuse me, ⁴_____ the police station?
      B It's on London Road. Take the first left and
         ⁵_____ the theatre. The police station is on ⁶_____.
   4 A ⁷_____ lend me a pencil, please?
      B Sure, there's one on my desk. Just take it.
   5 A Excuse me, is there a bank ⁸_____?
      B Yes, there's one on West Street. Go to the end of this street and ⁹_____. The bank is on the left.

31

5 Clothes and shopping

5.1 Shopping

Vocabulary shopping

1 Complete the crossword.

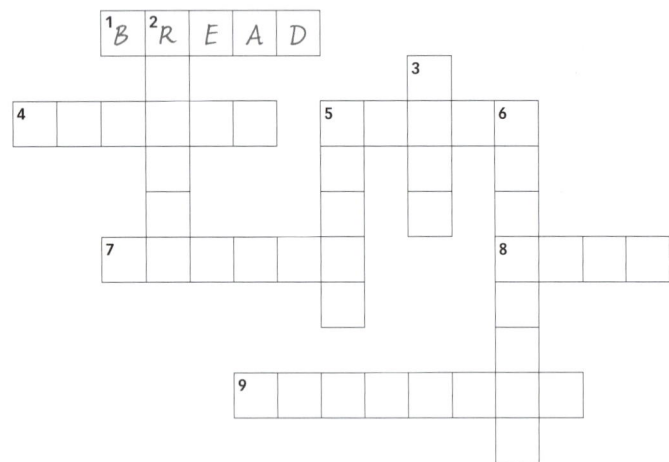

Across ▶
1 You get it at the baker's.
4 You buy things at a shopping _____.
5 You do this with money.
7 On the internet.
8 Money.
9 You buy one at the newsagent's.

Down ▼
2 You can usually _____ something you don't like to a shop.
3 The butcher's sells this.
5 A time when shops sell things at low prices.
6 There's a 20% _____ on everything today.

2 Choose the correct options to complete the article.

Shopping past and present

A few years ago you could drive to the centre of an American town, look at what was in the shops, get help from a shop assistant, and pay for things with ¹*cash* / *sales*. Today there are small food shops in some town centres, but most people don't buy their meat from a local ² *newsagent's / butcher's*, their daily newspaper from the local ³ *newsagent's / discount* or their bread from the local ⁴ *baker's / shopping centre*. They prefer to ⁵ *spend / cash* their money in big supermarkets or ⁶ *sales / shopping centres*, or they shop from home.

Now people do more and more shopping ⁷ *centres / online*. In 2012, it was 22% of food shopping and 37% of shopping for clothes, but every year it's more. Around 71% of American men and 66% of American women shop on the internet. It's very easy to find big ⁸ *cash / discounts* and save money. You don't need to stand outside and wait for shops to open in the ⁹ *sales / discounts*, and you can ¹⁰ *return / spend* things that you don't like.

32 | Oxford 3000™

Grammar can/can't/could/couldn't

3 Complete the sentences with the correct form of *can/could* and the verb in (brackets).

Now and Then

1 People _couldn't pay_ (not pay) for things with credit cards before 1958, but they _could pay_ (pay) with cash.
Today you _____ (buy) things with cash or credit cards in most shops, but you _____ (not use) cash to pay for things online.

2 Now you _____ (get) money from cash machines around the world or you _____ (go) into a bank.
Before 1967, you _____ (get) money from your bank but you _____ (not take) money from a cash machine.

3 Before 1994, you _____ (get) a computer and use the internet, but you _____ (not shop) online. Today there are some things that you _____ (not do) online – have a haircut, for example – but you _____ (find) most things that you need.

4 You _____ (have) a colour TV in 1953, but you _____ (not watch) a TV programme in colour. The first colour TV programme was in 1954! Today we _____ (enjoy) thousands of colour TV programmes from around the world. Most of today's young people _____ (not remember) black and white TV.

5 Before 1994 people _____ (eat) a meal in an English restaurant on Sundays, but they _____ (not buy) food from an English supermarket.
Today most supermarkets in the United Kingdom open seven days a week and they offer online shopping. When you _____ (not go) to the supermarket, you _____ (visit) their online store.

4 Rewrite the sentences as questions using *can/could*. Then complete the answers.

1 You could get cash from machines in the 1880s.
Could you get cash from machines in the 1880s?
Yes, you _could_.

2 He can visit the museum on Sunday.
_____
_____, he _____.

3 I can book the plane tickets online.
_____
_____, I _____.

4 We can't park in the centre of the town.
_____
_____, we _____.

5 People couldn't shop online in the 1980s.
_____
_____, they _____.

6 Children could play outside in the past.
_____
_____, they _____.

5 Correct the sentences.
1 Can you buys bread at the newsagent's?
Can you buy bread at the newsagent's?
2 Could people spending euros in 1995?
_____
3 A Can you do this exercise?
  B Yes, I can do.
  A _____
  B _____
4 You can't use the internet in 1975.
_____
5 You can't to swim in the sea – it's dangerous.
_____
6 People could buy most things online now.
_____

PRONUNCIATION can

6a 5.1))) Listen to the sentences. Look at the words in **bold**. Are they stressed (S) or unstressed (U)?
1 A **Can** we book the theatre tickets online? _U_
  B No, but we **can** book them by phone. ___
2 A **Can** he play a musical instrument? ___
  B Yes, he **can**. ___
3 A I **can't** pay with my credit card. ___
  B That's OK, you **can** pay with cash. ___
  A No, I **can't**. I haven't got any cash. ___

b 5.1))) Listen again. Pause the listening and repeat after each item. Copy the stress.

I can …	Very well	Quite well	More practice
talk about shopping.	○	○	○
use *can* and *could* to talk about possibility and ability.	○	○	○

33

5.2 What is he wearing?

Vocabulary clothes and accessories

1a Match the clothes and accessories to the pictures.
- coat   13
- dress   __
- glasses __
- gloves   __
- hat   __
- hoodie   __
- jacket   __
- jeans   __
- jewellery __
- scarf   __
- shoes   __
- shorts   __
- skirt   __
- socks   __
- suit   __
- tie   __
- top   __
- trainers __
- trousers __
- T-shirt __
- umbrella __

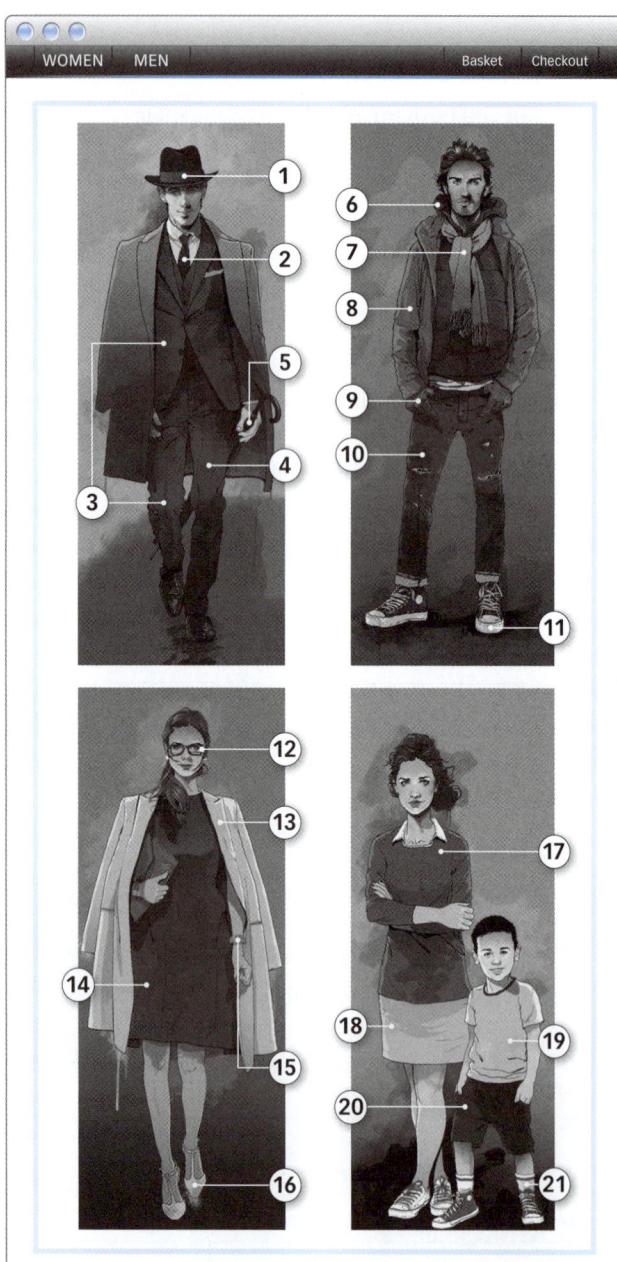

b 5.2)) Listen, check and repeat.

2 Choose the correct word.
1 It's raining – take *a scarf* / *an umbrella* / *a tie*.
2 Martha wears a lot of gold *jeans* / *jewellery* / *scarves*.
3 I need *glasses* / *ties* / *trainers* for reading.
4 Jenny's wearing a blue *sock* / *hoodie* / *suit* for her interview at the bank.
5 A My hands are really cold.
   B Wear your *T-shirt* / *coat* / *gloves*.
6 You wear a scarf round your *hands* / *feet* / *neck*.
7 She spends a lot of money on designer *hats* / *shoes* / *tops*, but she can't walk in them.
8 Wear your *coat* / *glasses* / *shorts* – it's cold outside.

Grammar present continuous

3 Complete the sentences. Use the present continuous form of a verb from the box.

~~buy~~ drive have make rain swim wear work

1 Deidre and Mick are in a shop. They *'re buying* a new white carpet for their bedroom.
2 Jim isn't at the office today. He_____ from home.
3 I like the yellow hat your mum_____ in your wedding photos.
4 A What are you doing?
   B I_____ a pizza for dinner.
5 A Are the kids upstairs?
   B No, they_____ in the pool.
6 A Is this room free?
   B No, I'm sorry it isn't. We_____ a meeting here.
7 Please slow down. You_____ very fast.
8 We can't go to the beach today – it_____ .

34 Oxford 3000™

4 Make negative (–) sentences and questions (?). Use the present continuous.
1 (?) where / Allen and Daria / go
   Where are Allen and Daria going?
2 (?) you / drink my coffee
3 (–) he / listen to the teacher
4 (?) Ellie / do her homework
5 (–) I / enjoy this film
6 (–) it / snow today / but it's cold
7 (?) why / those people / stand there
8 (–) we / work today

Grammar present continuous or present simple

5 Complete the sentences. Put one of the verbs in (brackets) in the present continuous and one of the verbs in the present simple.
1 I usually _drive_ to work, but today I'm taking the train. (drive / take)
2 Andrea _____ in an office from Monday to Friday but today is Saturday and she _____ at home. (work / relax)
3 Yanni _____ any clothes to wear for his job interview so he _____ a new suit. (buy / not have)
4 We _____ work now because it _____ half past five. (be / leave)
5 They _____ outside the shop – it _____ at nine o'clock. (wait / open)
6 A Why _____ you _____ to the bank?
   B Because I _____ to get some money from the cash machine. (go / want)
7 Sandy's in the shopping centre. She _____ some trousers to a shop because she _____ them. (return / not like)
8 A It _____ !
   B It's OK, I always _____ an umbrella in my bag. (rain / carry)

6 Read the text and look at the verbs in **bold**. Put six of the verbs into the present continuous.

An Indian wedding

Ashna ¹**lives** in Mumbai with her parents and her sisters, Meena and Lalita. Ashna ²**gets** married today. Meena and Lalita ³**help** their sister to get dressed for the wedding. In India, women usually ⁴**wear** a long dress called a sari for their wedding and they ⁵**paint** their hands with something red called 'kumkuma'. Today Ashna ⁶**wears** a red sari and a lot of gold jewellery.

This morning, Ashna's mother ⁷**checks** the food for the party after the wedding. She ⁸**enjoys** cooking, but today ⁹**is** a big day and she ¹⁰**needs** help. A lot of people ¹¹**come** to the house and so Ashna's aunts ¹²**cook** special food for them.

1 lives   ✓   7 checks   _____
2 gets   _is getting_   8 enjoys   _____
3 help   _____   9 is   _____
4 wear   _____   10 needs   _____
5 paint   _____   11 come   _____
6 wears   _____   12 cook   _____

I can …	Very well	Quite well	More practice
talk about clothes.	○	○	○
use the present continuous to talk about actions at the moment.	○	○	○

5.3 Vocabulary development

Vocabulary: adjectives and adverbs

1 Rewrite the sentences using the adverb form of the adjective in (brackets).

1. I can't run in these shoes. (fast)
   I can't run fast in these shoes.
2. Sylvia can't see without her glasses. (clear)
   _____
3. Peter and Jan work every day. (hard)
   _____
4. I always drive. (careful)
   _____
5. Why do the trains always arrive? (late)
   _____
6. Please play. (quiet)
   _____
7. My sister cooks. (good)
   _____

2 Choose the correct options.
1. This is a (slow) / slowly train.
2. I don't speak French very good / well.
3. Please don't drive dangerous / dangerously in the rain.
4. What's the correct / correctly answer to question six?
5. Children, please be quiet / quietly.
6. Why are you walking quick / quickly? We have lots of time.
7. All my friends say that I sing really bad / badly!

Vocabulary review

3 Match the words to the definitions.

| the baker's   the butcher's   cash   a discount |
| the newsagent's   ~~online~~   return   the sales |
| shopping centre   spend |

1. A way to shop from your own home.   _online_
2. You use it to pay for things.   _____
3. You do this with money and time.   _____
4. A place with a lot of shops.   _____
5. A shop that sells bread.   _____
6. A shop that sells newspapers.   _____
7. Take back something you don't like to a shop.   _____
8. The time of year when shops sell things cheaply.   _____
9. A shop that sells meat.   _____
10. Something you get when you buy something during the sales.   _____

4 Write the words in the correct column.

| ~~coat~~   dress   ~~glasses~~   gloves   hat   hoodie   jacket |
| jeans   jewellery   scarf   shoes   skirt   socks   suit   tie |
| top   trainers   trousers   T-shirt   umbrella |

Clothes	Accessories
coat	glasses

5 Complete the table.

Adjective	Adverb	Adjective	Adverb
bad	¹ _badly_	good	⁷ _____
² _____	carefully	⁸ _____	hard
clear	³ _____	⁹ _____	late
⁴ _____	dangerously	quick	¹⁰ _____
⁵ _____	easily	quiet	¹¹ _____
fast	⁶ _____	¹² _____	slowly

Oxford 3000™

5.4 Speaking and writing

Speaking in a shop

1 Complete the conversation between a customer (C) and an assistant (A). Use the words in the boxes.

| credit card | discount | ~~excuse~~ | help | how much | off | take |

1 C ¹ _Excuse_ me?
  A Yes? How can I ² _____ you?
  C ³ _____ is this scarf?
  A It's £9.99.
  C Do you do a student ⁴ _____ ?
  A Yes, we do. You get 10% ⁵ _____ with a student card.
  C Oh, that's good. Can I pay by ⁶ _____ ?
  A No, I'm afraid we only ⁷ _____ cash.

| ask | ~~can~~ | changing rooms | close | just | need | try |

2 A ¹ _Can_ I help you?
  C No, thanks. I'm ² _____ looking.
  A Well if you ³ _____ anything, just ⁴ _____ .
  C What time do you ⁵ _____ ?
  A At half past six.
  C Can I ⁶ _____ on this top, please?
  A Yes, of course. The ⁷ _____ are on the left, behind the jeans.

2a Put the assistant's phrases in the correct place in the conversation.
- And would you like your receipt in the bag?
- That's £4.50, please.
- What kind do you want?
- Would you like a bag?

C Do you sell batteries?
A Yes, we do. ¹ _____
C Er … AAA, please – they're for my camera.
A ² _____
C Can I have two packets?
A That's £9.00. ³ _____
C Yes, please. Just a small one.
A ⁴ _____
C Yes, please.

b 5.4))) Listen, check and repeat each line of the conversation.

➔ **STUDY TIP** Practise listen-and-repeat exercises several times with the words in front of you, then try covering the words and practising the exercise again to see how much you remember.

Writing a product review

3 Change this bad review into a good review. Use the words in the box.

| easy | expensive | great value | ~~I recommend it~~ | quickly |

WRITE A REVIEW | READ MORE REVIEWS

★★★★☆

This is a great bike and ¹**I'm very disappointed with it**. It's only £150, but it looks ²**cheap**. It's also very ³**difficult** to use. So overall, it's ⁴**not worth the money**. It arrived ⁵**two weeks late**, too on the day after I ordered it.

1 _I recommend it_ _____
2 _____
3 _____
4 _____
5 _____

4 Put commas and *and* into these sentences.
1 She's wearing a scarf a hat gloves today.
  _____
  _____

2 Shopping online is easy cheap you can return things that you don't like.
  _____
  _____

3 Jake's a good driver: he drives slowly carefully not too fast.
  _____
  _____

I can …	Very well	Quite well	More practice
use adverbs.	○	○	○
buy things in a shop.	○	○	○
write an online product review.	○	○	○

37

6 The past

6.1 Don't give up!

Grammar *was* and *were*

1 Make positive (+) or negative (–) sentences, or questions (?) using the past form of *be*.
1 (+) the co-founders of Microsoft / Bill Gates and Paul Allen   _The co-founders of Microsoft were Bill Gates and Paul Allen._
2 (?) the restaurant / expensive
3 (–) Harry's meal / very good
4 (+) I / very tired last night
5 (?) where / you / yesterday
6 (–) we / late for work this morning
7 (?) why / Vincent van Gogh / famous
8 (–) I / born in England

2 Choose the correct options to complete the article.

IKEA is born

Ingvar Kamprad ¹(was)/ were the founder of the furniture company IKEA. He ² was / were born in 1926 in Sweden. His parents ³ wasn't / weren't rich – they ⁴ was / were farmers and the family home ⁵ was / were near a small village in the south of Sweden. Ingvar ⁶ wasn't / weren't interested in farming. He started IKEA in his uncle's kitchen in 1943. His first products ⁷ was / were pencils and other small items. There ⁸ wasn't / weren't any IKEA stores before 1958 – it ⁹ was / were only possible to buy things from IKEA by mail. The first IKEA store ¹⁰ was / were in Sweden, but now there are stores around the world.

3 Read the article in exercise **2** again. Complete the questions below with *was* or *were*, then write short answers.
1 _Was_ Ingvar Kamprad born in Sweden?
  Yes, he was.
2 _____ his parents rich?
  _____
3 _____ they farmers?
  _____
4 _____ Ingvar interested in farming?
  _____
5 _____ IKEA furniture on sale in 1950?
  _____

PRONUNCIATION the past of *to be*

4a Are the words in **bold** stressed (S) or unstressed (U)?
1 I **was** tired last night. _U_
2 **Was** I tired last night? ___
3 Yes, I **was**. ___
4 No, I **wasn't**. ___
5 They **were** at home last night. ___
6 **Were** they at home last night? ___
7 Yes, they **were**. ___
8 No, they **weren't**. ___

38 Oxford 3000™

b **6.1** 🔊 Listen and check.

c **6.1** 🔊 Listen again. Pause the listening and repeat after each sentence.

5a **6.2** 🔊 Listen to the pronunciation of *was/were*. Write stressed (S) or unstressed (U).
1 A Was Elvis Presley famous? _U_
   B Yes, he was. ___
2 A Why was the doctor at your house? ___
   B My husband was sick. ___
3 A Where were you yesterday? ___
   B We were at work. ___
4 A Were the teachers at your first school nice? ___
   B Yes, they were. ___
5 A When were you born? ___
   B I was born in 1992. ___

b **6.2** 🔊 Listen again. Pause the listening and repeat after each sentence.

Vocabulary   time expressions

6 Put the words in the right order to make sentences.
1 her / Jackie / in / hour / ago / was / office / an / half .
   Jackie was in her office half an hour ago.
2 in / London Olympics / The / 2012 / were / last .
   _____
3 There / night / was / match / an / last / football / important .
   _____
4 year / Spain / We / in / were / last .
   _____
5 morning / was / tired / I / this / very .
   _____
6 Albert Einstein / nineteenth / in / century / born / the / was .
   _____
7 a / staff meeting / few / There / days / was / ago / a .
   _____
8 in hospital / She / two / ago / was / months .
   _____

7 Look at the events in exercise 6. Put them in order, with the most recent event first.
   NOW
1 _Jackie was in her office half an hour ago._
2 _____
3 _____
4 _____
5 _____
6 _____
7 _____
8 _____

8 Complete the text. Use the word/phrase/date in (brackets) and add *in*, *last* or *ago*.

FAMILY HISTORY

My father-in-law, Glen, was a police officer, but he retired [1] _in 2006_ (2006). Now, he has more time and he enjoys researching his family history. Glen goes to family-history meetings every month and he visits museums all over the country to find out more information about his own family – [2] _____ (month) he was in York and this week he's in Cambridge.

[3] _____ (two years), he was in Wales. He was there because [4] _____ (the 19th century) his grandparents were farmers in Wales. It was [5] _____ (a long time), but the farm is there today! [6] _____ (year) he was in Canada – Glen's aunt moved to Canada [7] _____ (1935) and Glen has some cousins in Toronto. He was really happy to meet them when he was there [8] _____ (the summer). My husband and I were at Glen's house [9] _____ (night) and he showed us his photos of Wales and Canada – they were very interesting.

I can ...	Very well	Quite well	More practice
use *was/were* to talk about the past.	○	○	○
use other time expressions.	○	○	○

6.2 Stories

Grammar past simple regular verbs

1 Write the past simple for each of the verbs.
   1 carry   _carried_
   2 close   _____
   3 collect _____
   4 copy   _____
   5 earn   _____
   6 enjoy   _____
   7 look   _____
   8 love   _____
   9 play   _____
   10 relax _____
   11 return _____
   12 try   _____

2 Complete the article. Use the past simple of the verbs in (brackets).

THE STORY OF THE CASHPOINT

There weren't any cash machines (sometimes called 'cash points') until the 1960s. When people ¹ _wanted_ (want) to take out money from their bank, they usually ² _____ (visit) the bank and ³ _____ (wait) in a line to speak to one of the bank workers. Banks ⁴ _____ (open) during the week and on Saturday mornings. This was a problem if you ⁵ _____ (need) money at any other time.

John Shepherd-Barron ⁶ _____ (study) at the University of Cambridge and he ⁷ _____ (work) for De La Rue, a company that made banknotes for different countries. One day, John ⁸ _____ (arrive) at his bank, but it was closed and he couldn't get any money. He ⁹ _____ (notice) the vending machines that people ¹⁰ _____ (use) to buy drinks and food and he ¹¹ _____ (decide) that it was possible to have a 'money vending machine'. He ¹² _____ (talk) to Barclays – a British bank – and they ¹³ _____ (like) his idea. That was in 1965. Today there are over two million cash machines around the world.

3 Choose one word to complete each sentence and write it in the past simple.
   1 live / look / close
     I _lived_ in Bangladesh when I was a child.
   2 change / believe / prepare
     The Lobi people of ancient Ghana _____ snake money helped them to stay safe.
   3 watch / listen / enjoy
     We _____ to the radio when we were in the car.
   4 start / practise / collect
     Sally _____ her new job last week.
   5 copy / hurry / carry
     Sam _____ the shopping to his car.
   6 retire / return / turn
     Dan doesn't work now – he _____ when he was sixty-five.
   7 use / turn / pay
     In the past, people _____ for things with salt.

PRONUNCIATION -ed ending in past simple verbs

4a Circle the verb which doesn't have the same -ed sound.
   1 /d/   changed / returned / (started)
   2 /t/   called / looked / thanked
   3 /ɪd/ collected / finished / included
   4 /t/   worked / liked / posted
   5 /d/   believed / noticed / prepared
   6 /ɪd/ wanted / needed / used
   7 /d/   waited / received / moved
   8 /ɪd/ responded / watched / shouted
   9 /t/   noticed / practised / turned

b 6.3))) Listen and check.

c 6.3))) Listen again and repeat.

→ **STUDY TIP** When you learn a new verb, write down in your notebook if it's regular or irregular. For regular verbs, write down the pronunciation, using the symbols in exercise 4a. For irregular verbs, write down the past simple form, and try to learn it at the same time.

Vocabulary: common regular verb collocations

5 Match the beginnings and endings of the collocations.

1 prepare a — g meal
2 receive an — e email
3 move — d house
4 post a — f letter
5 shout at — h someone
6 visit a — c relative
7 enter a — b competition
8 wait — a for a long time

6 Complete the conversations with a collocation from exercise **5**. Use the past simple form.

1 **A** Does Molly still live in Manchester?
   B No, she _moved house_ last year. She lives in Birmingham now.

2 **A** You're late again, Mary.
   B I know, I'm sorry. There were no buses this morning – I _____, then I decided to walk.

3 **A** How was your birthday?
   B Great! We stayed at home and Daniel _____. It was very nice.
   A What did he cook?

4 **A** Tony _____ for a new car last week.
   B Really? I hope he wins!

5 **A** How's Rim?
   B She's fine. I _____ from her yesterday. She's living in Saudi Arabia now.
   A Can you give me her new address so I can write to her?
   B Of course.

6 **A** I can't remember the last time I _____.
   B I can! It was a few weeks ago when Jamie showed you his pet snake. You were really angry.
   A That's because Jamie knows that I don't like snakes.

7 **A** How long does it take for a postcard to get from here to Australia?
   B About seven days, I think. My cousin _____ to me from Sydney last week and it arrived here yesterday.

8 **A** When was the last time you _____?
   B Two months ago – all of my family live in Poland and I only see them three or four times a year.

I can …	Very well	Quite well	More practice
use regular verbs to talk about what happened in the past.	○	○	○
use common collocations.	○	○	○

6.3 Vocabulary development

Vocabulary: adverbs of degree

1 Put the adverbs of degree in (brackets) into the sentences.
   1 There are a lot of old buildings in the city. (very)
      There are a lot of very old buildings in the city.
   2 It's common to see tourists in my town. (quite)
   3 The palace that we visited was interesting. (really)
   4 The tour guide's talk was boring. (a bit)
   5 The people in the hotel were unfriendly. (very)
   6 The seats on the bus were uncomfortable. (a bit)
   7 It's cold here in winter. (really)
   8 It's expensive to have a holiday in England. (quite)

2 Choose the best options to complete the sentences.
   1 The museum was *a bit* / *very* boring, but it was OK – I saw some interesting things there.
   2 His French is *a bit* / *quite* good, but he doesn't understand everything.
   3 I think tourism is *really* / *a bit* important for our town.
   4 Steve Jobs, the founder of Apple computers, was a *bit* / *very* successful businessman.
   5 The tickets for the art exhibition were *a bit* / *quite* cheap.
   6 I like my new boss. She's *very* / *quite* friendly.
   7 It's *really* / *a bit* hot today – the temperature is 39°C.
   8 We were *a bit* / *really* late – we arrived five minutes after the start of the film.

   PRONUNCIATION sentence stress

3a 6.4))) Listen to the sentences. Underline the stressed words.
   1 He's a bit unfriendly.
   2 Those bags are quite cheap.
   3 She's really friendly.
   4 This is a very interesting article.

b 6.4))) Listen again. Pause the listening and repeat after each sentence.

Vocabulary review

4 Write the time expressions in the correct column.

| 1974 2011 a long time night the sixteenth century |
| the summer three months two weeks week year |

in	last	ago
the sixteenth century		

5 Complete the collocations. Use words/phrases from the box.

| a competition an email house a letter a long time |
| a meal a relative someone |

   1 enter _a competition_
   2 move _____
   3 post _____
   4 prepare _____
   5 receive _____
   6 shout at _____
   7 visit _____
   8 wait _____

6 Put the sentences in the correct order from strong to weak.

| It's a bit cold. It's quite hot. It's really boring. |
| It's very expensive. |

   100%
   1 _____ / _____
   2 _____
   3 _____
   0%

6.4 Speaking and writing

Speaking showing interest as a listener

1 Read the sentences in each column. Write *good news, bad news* or *interesting news* at the top of each column.

1 _____	2 _____	3 _____
The train is late again.	I'm starting a salsa class tomorrow.	It's my daughter's wedding next week.
My boss is really angry with me.	Tom had an interview yesterday.	Emma passed her driving test!
Mark's grandfather died last week.	There's a Turkish film on TV tonight.	It's stopped raining – we can go to the beach!

2a Read the phrases. Are they responses to good news, responses to bad news or responses to interesting news?

1 That's awful! — *bad news*
2 What a nightmare! _____
3 Really? _____
4 That's great! _____
5 That's terrible! _____
6 That's amazing! _____
7 Poor you! _____
8 That's brilliant! _____
9 Oh no! _____

b 6.5))) Listen and say the phrases. Copy the intonation.

3a Choose the best way to complete the conversations.
1 A My interview went really well. They offered me the job.
  B (That's brilliant!)/ Really?
2 A Julia and Mark are getting married.
  B That's great! / That's awful!
3 A Our new neighbours moved into the house next door yesterday.
  B Really? / That's amazing!
4 A I've got a cold.
  B That's amazing! / Poor you!

5 A The bus is late again.
  B Oh no! / That's brilliant!
6 A Our holiday was terrible! The hotel was awful, the people were really unfriendly and it rained every day so we couldn't go to the beach.
  B What a nightmare! / Really?
7 A My grandfather is 102 years old today.
  B That's terrible! / That's amazing!
8 A Ken is really unhappy. The company he worked for closed last week and now he's unemployed.
  B That's brilliant! / That's awful!

b 6.6))) Listen to the first part of the conversation and say the response, then listen and check.

Writing write a tweet or a text message

4a Put the missing words in the tweets to make full sentences.

1 👤 Want to go to Istanbul in April. Anyone know a good hotel there?

2 👤 Watching a great programme about famous singers. Anyone else watching it?

3 👤 Just waited an hour for the bus! So boring!

b Match replies a-c to tweets 1-3. Cross out the unnecessary words.

a 👤 Poor you! ~~Are you~~ home now? ~~Do you~~ want to meet for coffee later? ___

b 👤 Really?! I only watched 5 minutes. It was awful! ___

c 👤 Try Hotel Empress Zoe. I went there last year. It's really beautiful. ___

I can …	Very well	Quite well	More practice
show interest as a listener.	○	○	○
write a tweet or a text message.	○	○	○
use adverbs of degree.	○	○	○

43

6.5 Listening for pleasure

A guided tour of Stratford-upon-Avon

1 Complete the text about William Shakespeare.

> 1616　films　plays　town　~~writer~~

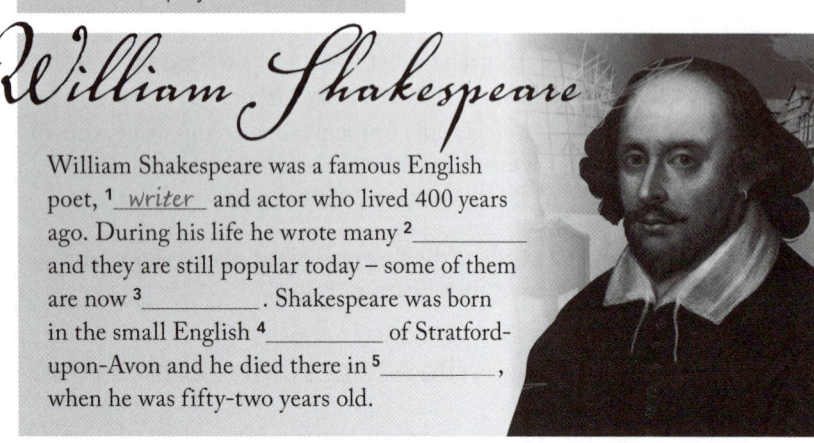

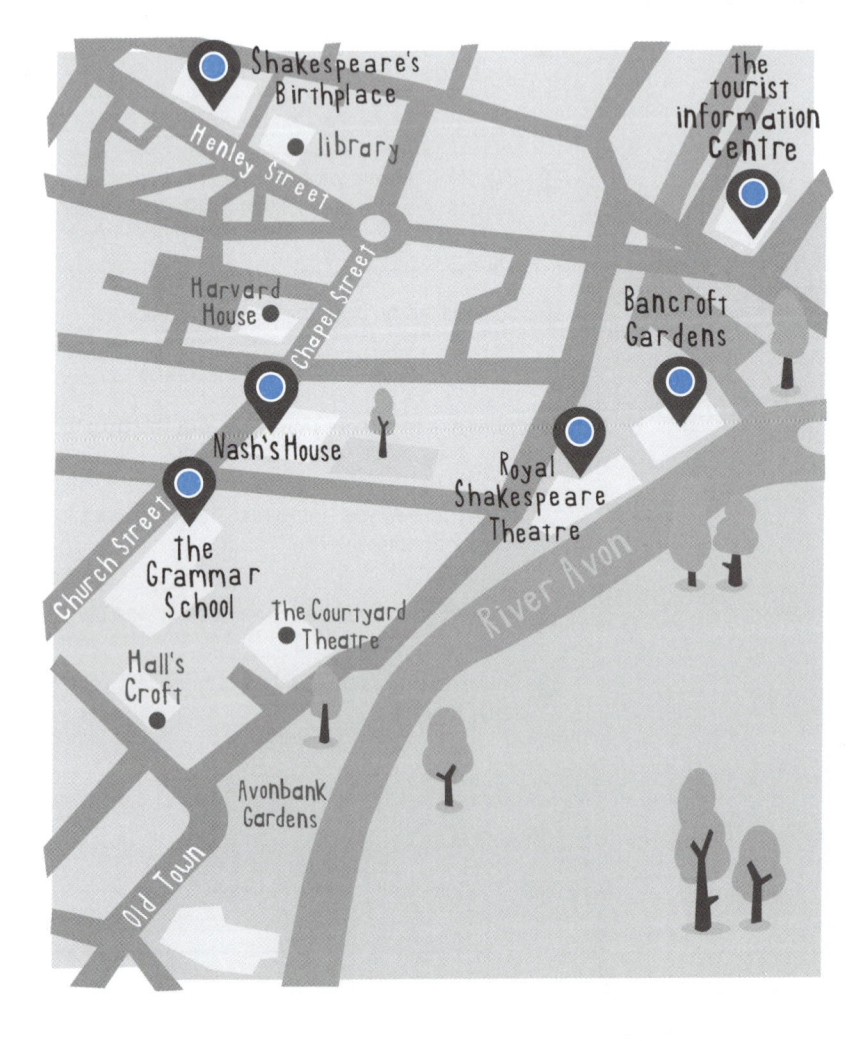

William Shakespeare

William Shakespeare was a famous English poet, [1] _writer_ and actor who lived 400 years ago. During his life he wrote many [2] _____ and they are still popular today – some of them are now [3] _____. Shakespeare was born in the small English [4] _____ of Stratford-upon-Avon and he died there in [5] _____, when he was fifty-two years old.

2 Match the places in blue on the map to the definitions. Check any new words in your dictionary.
  1 The place where Shakespeare was born.
     Shakespeare's birthplace
  2 A place where you can watch a play.
     _____
  3 A place where children go to learn.
     _____
  4 A place where you can sit outside and relax.
     _____
  5 A place where visitors to Stratford-upon-Avon can find information.
     _____
  6 A house where someone called Nash lived.
     _____

3 6.7))) Listen to a podcast describing a walk around the centre of Stratford-upon-Avon.

4 Look at the map and complete the tour description with the names of the places.

> We really enjoyed our tour of Stratford-upon-Avon. We started at the [1] _tourist information centre_ and walked to [2] _____ in Henley Street. Then we walked to [3] _____ on Chapel Street. This was the home of Shakespeare's granddaughter.
>
> Our next stop was the [4] _____ on Church Street. Shakespeare was a student here. After that we visited Hall's Croft, which is on a street called Old Town. This is the house that Shakespeare's daughter lived in. We then had a walk along the river and our next stop was the [6] _____, which is quite a modern building. The tour finished in [7] _____. It was lovely to sit there and have an ice cream.

Oxford 3000™

Review: Units 5 and 6

Grammar

1 Choose the correct form.
   1 Martine is at the newsagent's. She *buys* / *('s buying)* a newspaper.
   2 *Could* / *Can* you drive when you were seventeen?
   3 I'm sorry I *couldn't* / *can't* phone you yesterday. I didn't have my phone.
   4 Jim's car is at the garage so he *takes* / *'s taking* the bus to town today.
   5 I can't talk to you now – I *'m working* / *work*.
   6 You *can* / *could* use credit cards in most shops now.
   7 We *don't usually pay* / *'m not usually paying* for things with cash.
   8 A Mark's in the kitchen.
     B What *does he cook* / *is he cooking*?
   9 Tanya was busy and she couldn't *to go* / *go* to the meeting.
   10 My children *don't like* / *aren't liking* their new teacher.

2 Complete the article with the past simple form of the verbs in (brackets). Use contractions where possible.

Before the internet

It's difficult to believe that just over twenty years ago the internet [1] *wasn't* (not be) here for us to use. When the internet started there [2] _____ (not be) many people with home computers – most people [3] _____ (use) internet cafés to go online and check their emails or to play games and the cafés [4] _____ (be) quite expensive to use.

Today the internet plays an important part in our lives and we can't imagine life without it. We shop online, find information, chat and play games with people around the world. Life [5] _____ (be) very different for our parents. They [6] _____ (walk) into shops to do their shopping, they [7] _____ (look) for information in books to find the answers to their questions, they [8] _____ (chat) to friends in the street or on the phone and they [9] _____ (play) games at home with their families.

[10] _____ (be) things better in the past or are they better now?

Vocabulary

3 Complete the conversations with words from the box.

baker's   bit   blue   discount   glasses   gloves   ~~money~~
really   return   sales   shoes   top

   1 A How much *money* do you spend on clothes?
     B I don't spend a lot – I usually buy my clothes in the _____ .
   2 A This red dress is _____ nice.
     B I prefer the _____ one.
   3 A I bought these designer _____ online, but I can't walk in them.
     B Can you _____ them and get your money back?
   4 A I like the _____ you're wearing.
     B Thanks – I bought it last week. It was cheap because I got a 40% _____ .
   5 A My hands are a _____ cold.
     B Why don't you wear your _____ ?
   6 A Is that a _____ over there? I need to buy some bread.
     B I don't know. I can't see what the sign says without my _____ .

4 Choose the correct options.
   1 We moved *house* / *the house* last year.
   2 Did you *wait the bus* / *wait for the bus* for a long time?
   3 I retired *long time ago* / *a long time ago*.
   4 The hotel is *a bit nice* / *very nice*.
   5 Julia works very *hard* / *hardly*.
   6 Ian drives *dangerous* / *dangerously*.
   7 Did you *post* / *enter* my letter yesterday?
   8 Were you at university *last* / *in* 2005?

Speaking

5 Complete the conversation with words from the box.

changing rooms   ~~help~~   looking   need   try

A Can I [1] *help* you?
B No, thanks. I'm just [2] _____ .
A Well, just ask if you [3] _____ anything.
B Excuse me. Can I [4] _____ this suit on, please?
A Yes, of course. The [5] _____ are over there.

45

7 Health and fitness

7.1 My health, my business

Vocabulary a healthy lifestyle

1 Choose the correct verb to complete the healthy living phrases.
 1 *sleep* / take seven to eight hours a night
 2 put / do physical jobs around the house
 3 ride / drive a bicycle
 4 have / walk to work
 5 go / take the stairs, not the lift
 6 eat / take lots of fruit and vegetables
 7 do / be an hour of exercise each day
 8 put / drink eight glasses of water a day
 9 see / go to the gym

2 Match the illustrations to the phrases from exercise 1.

 a _7_ b ___ c ___
 d ___ e ___ f ___
 g ___ h ___ i ___

3 Complete the article with seven phrases from exercise 1.

Small changes for a healthier life

FOOD
Try to eat more healthily, for example
¹ _eat lots of fruit and vegetables_ – doctors say that seven a day is a good number. And
² _____ – that's about two litres a day.

EXERCISE
It can be expensive to ³_____ and sometimes it's difficult to go every day, but there are other types of exercise you can do. On work days you can leave your car at home and
⁴_____ or ride a bike – you save money and you feel good. When you arrive at the office ⁵_____, to your floor. Walking up and down stairs for an hour uses over 500 calories (that's about the number of calories in a big hamburger!). After work, you can use more calories when you arrive home – don't sit in front of the TV, ⁶_____ or in the garden.

RELAXING
You don't feel healthy when you're tired.
⁷_____ – go to bed early and don't eat a big meal late in the evening.

→ **STUDY TIP** When you are reading in English, look for groups of words that are used together, for example *ride a bike*, *do exercise*, *take the stairs* – these are collocations. Make a note of them in your notebook and learn them as phrases, not individual words.

46 | Oxford 3000™

7.1 7.2 7.3 7.4

Grammar past simple irregular verbs

4a Complete the sentences. Use the past simple form of a verb from the box.

borrow live pay play ~~ride~~ sleep spend stop

1 We _rode_ our bikes to school when we were children.
2 She _____ money from the bank for her university fees.
3 When my parents were young, they _____ in South Africa.
4 Phil _____ football with his friends on Saturday.
5 They _____ for the meal with a credit card.
6 John _____ work at half past five and went home.
7 I don't know why you're tired – you _____ for ten hours last night.
8 I don't have any money – I _____ it all yesterday.

b Look at the verbs from exercise 4a. Do they have a regular past form or an irregular past form?

1 _rode – irregular_   5 _____
2 _____   6 _____
3 _____   7 _____
4 _____   8 _____

5 Write the verbs and their past form in the correct column. There are 12 regular verbs and 12 irregular verbs.

| ~~believe~~ ~~buy~~ catch change come copy drink fly
get hear leave like look put reduce show sit
study take tidy use want watch write |
|---|

Verbs with regular past simple forms	Verbs with irregular past simple forms
believe – believed	buy – bought

PRONUNCIATION past simple irregular verbs

6a 7.1))) Listen to the pronunciation of the groups of three past simple verbs. Circle the verb with a different vowel sound.
1 taught / bought /(rode)   4 came / drank / sang
2 chose / put / wrote   5 took / flew / put
3 said / felt / heard   6 made / ate / caught

b 7.1))) Listen again and repeat.

7 Complete the blog. Use the past simple form of the verbs in (brackets).

From this …

… to this in nine weeks!

My parents ¹ _had_ (have) a house near the beach when I was a child and my brother and I ² _____ (swim) every day. We also played tennis and we even ³ _____ (win) some tennis competitions. However, when I ⁴ _____ (leave) home, this all changed!

I joined a gym to keep fit, but I never ⁵ _____ (go). I ⁶ _____ (drive) everywhere and I ⁷ _____ (eat) a lot of the wrong food. I was very unfit.

My best friend, James, ⁸ _____ (tell) me about a nine-week running plan called Couch to 5K. He ⁹ _____ (say) that the plan was the idea of a runner called Josh Clark – Josh ¹⁰ _____ (think) running was a good way to help his mum.

I ¹¹ _____ (find) more information about Couch to 5K on the internet and decided to try it. In the first week I walked for five minutes, then I ¹² _____ (do) twenty minutes of walking and running. In week 9, I ¹³ _____ (run) for thirty minutes without stopping three times a week and I ¹⁴ _____ (feel) great! Now I love running – last week I ¹⁵ _____ (do) a ten-kilometre race!

Read my blog to find out more!

I can …	Very well	Quite well	More practice
use collocations for a healthy lifestyle.	○	○	○
use past simple irregular verbs.	○	○	○

47

7.2 Sporting heroes

Vocabulary sports and fitness

1a Write the words in the correct column.

| athletics | basketball | cycle | fishing | football | to the gym |
| jog | judo | run | ski | swim | tennis | yoga |

Verb	Go +	Play +	Do +
jog			

b 7.2))) Listen, check and repeat.

2 Which activities from exercise **1a** are in photos 1–8?

1 _____
2 _____
3 _____
4 _____ 
5 _____
6 _____
7 _____
8 _____

3 Match the beginnings and endings of the sentences.

1 Evening classes are a good idea if you want to learn
2 For me, the best reason to do sport is to have
3 We don't play football for fun – we play to
4 Exercise is the best way to lose
5 I cycle to work every day to keep
6 I joined a tennis club to make new

a fit.
b weight.
c friends.
d something new.
e win.
f fun.

Grammar past simple negative

4 Circle the correct answer: a, b or c.
1 The train didn't ___ on time this morning.
   a arrived   b to arrive   c arrive
2 They did ___ play football last weekend.
   a no   b not   c not to
3 It was cold here last week, but it ___.
   a didn't rained b didn't rain   c didn't to rain
4 Nigel didn't ___ to work yesterday.
   a go   b went   c goes
5 We ___ yoga yesterday.
   a didn't   b did do not   c didn't do
6 I ___ Sammy at the basketball game.
   a didn't see   b didn't saw   c saw not
7 You didn't ___ to the meeting this afternoon.
   a to come   b came   c come

48 Oxford 3000™

5 Make the sentences negative.

1 They went to Mexico.
   They didn't go to Mexico.
2 We stayed in a hotel.
3 The weather was very good.
4 He won the competition.
5 You were late for work.
6 I skied at the weekend.

6 Complete the pairs of sentences. Use one positive form and one negative form.

1 **buy a hat** ✓   **buy designer shoes** ✗
   She _bought_ a hat for the wedding.
   She _didn't buy_ designer shoes for the wedding.

2 **go shopping** ✗   **go fishing** ✓
   Dan _____ shopping.
   He _____ fishing.

3 **do judo** ✗   **do karate** ✓
   They _____ judo last night.
   They _____ karate.

4 **take the bus** ✓   **take the train** ✗
   We _____ the bus to Manchester.
   We _____ the train.

5 **lend me £20** ✗   **lend me £10** ✓
   You _____ me £20.
   You _____ me £10.

6 **start at half past two** ✗   **start at two o'clock** ✓
   The staff meeting _____ at half past two.
   It _____ at two o'clock.

7 **play basketball** ✓   **play football** ✗
   They _____ basketball.
   They _____ football.

7 Complete the article with the correct form of the verbs in (brackets).

Tegla Loroupe
Olympic runner

Tegla Loroupe was born in Kenya in 1973. She ¹ _started_ (start) school when she was seven. Her family ² _____ (not live) near the school, so Tegla ³ _____ (run) ten kilometres every morning to get to the school.

Tegla ⁴ _____ (want) to be a runner, but her father ⁵ _____ (not think) it was a good thing for a girl to do. Tegla ⁶ _____ (not agree) and she ⁷ _____ (not stop) running. Tegla was very successful in races all around the world during the 1990s and she ⁸ _____ (begin) to be very famous. In 2000, Tegla ⁹ _____ (enter) the marathon at the Sydney Olympics, but she wasn't well the night before the race and she ¹⁰ _____ (not win) a medal.

Tegla ¹¹ _____ (not want) to be just a runner. She ¹² _____ (decide) to help people in her part of Africa. In 2003, Tegla ¹³ _____ (start) an organization called the Tegla Loroupe Peace Foundation. She also ¹⁴ _____ (open) a school (the Tegla Loroupe Peace Academy) and a home for children who ¹⁵ _____ (not have) parents. Today she continues to work to help people around the world to have better lives.

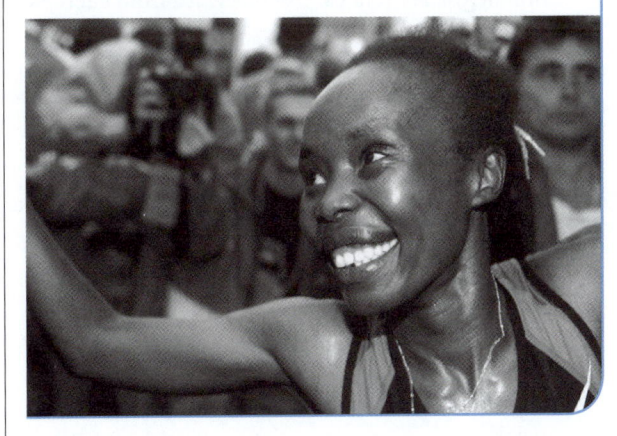

I can ...	Very well	Quite well	More practice
talk about sports and fitness.	○	○	○
use the past simple negative.	○	○	○

49

7.3 Vocabulary development

Vocabulary: easily confused words

1 Which sentence is correct? Tick (✓) a or b.
1. a Do you enjoy looking at photos? ✓
   b Do you enjoy watching photos?
2. a It's raining. Bring an umbrella when you go out.
   b It's raining. Take an umbrella when you go out.
3. a Jeff went to bed early. He said that he was tired.
   b Jeff went to bed early. He told that he was tired.
4. a Can you borrow me some money for a taxi?
   b Can you lend me some money for a taxi?
5. a We stayed at home and looked at TV last night.
   b We stayed at home and watched TV last night.
6. a Can you take me that newspaper?
   b Can you bring me that newspaper?
7. a We lent money from the bank to buy our house.
   b We borrowed money from the bank to buy our house.
8. a Come over here and look at this picture.
   b Go over here and look at this picture.
9. a You didn't tell me about your new job.
   b You didn't say me about your new job.
10. a I'm going home – it's five o'clock. See you tomorrow.
    b I'm coming home – it's five o'clock. See you tomorrow.

2 Complete the sentences. Use one word from each pair of words in the box.

| borrowed / lent   brought / took   looked at / watched |
| said / told   went / came |

1. Jack _told_ me that he didn't like his new boss.
2. We _____ to Thailand last year. We had a great time there.
3. They didn't have any money for food so I _____ them $10.
4. She _____ a lot of clothes in the shop, but she didn't buy anything.
5. My grandchildren _____ me to the theatre last week.

Vocabulary review

3 Complete the phrases about healthy living.

| do (x2)   drink   eat   go   ride   sleep   take   walk |

1. _walk_ to work
2. _____ the stairs, not the lift
3. _____ a bicycle
4. _____ an hour of exercise each day
5. _____ seven to eight hours a night
6. _____ lots of fruit and vegetables
7. _____ eight glasses of water a day
8. _____ to the gym or an evening class
9. _____ physical jobs around the house

4 Add *do*, *play*, *go* or (–) to each group of activities.
1. _____ basketball, football, tennis
2. _____ athletics, judo, yoga
3. _____ fishing, to the gym
4. _____ cycle, jog, run, ski, swim

5 Choose the correct verb to complete the phrases.
1. to (have) / keep fun
2. to win / keep fit
3. to meet / learn something new
4. to lose / win weight
5. to meet / win friends
6. to win / have a competition

6 Match the pairs of easily confused words, then translate them into your language.

| go   lend   take   tell   watch |

1. a bring   _____
   b _take_   _____
2. a borrow   _____
   b _____   _____
3. a come   _____
   b _____   _____
4. a look at   _____
   b _____   _____
5. a say   _____
   b _____   _____

50   Oxford 3000™

7.4 Speaking and writing

Speaking — opinions, agreeing and disagreeing

1a Complete the conversations. Use the phrases in the boxes.

> I agree   I don't know about that   I think
> What's your opinion   Yes, but

a A ¹ _What's your opinion_ of video exercise games?
   B They're OK. I've got a dance video that I use sometimes.
   A My kids want one of those tennis games – they say the games are a good way to keep fit, but ² _____. They can play tennis in the park.
   B ³ _____ only in the summer! With a video game you can exercise inside all year.
   A That's true, but ⁴ _____ children today spend a lot of time in front of computer and TV screens and they need to do more things outside. Things were different when we were kids.
   B ⁵ _____ with you. But the world is a different place now.

> I don't agree   I don't know about that   for me
> That's right   What do you think

b A ¹ _____ of this company in London? They use mobile phone technology to check what their workers eat, when they exercise and how they sleep. And they also give them an exercise plan. I think it's a great idea.
   B ² _____ with you.
   A Why not?
   B Well, ³ _____, people's health is their business.
   A ⁴ _____. When people aren't healthy, they can't work and companies lose money.
   B ⁵ _____, of course. But do people really want their bosses to tell them what to eat and when to exercise?
   A Maybe not.

b 7.3))) Listen and check.

2 Put the phrases in the box next to the correct heading. Use the conversations in exercise **1a** to help you.

> For me, …   I agree (with that).   I don't know about that.
> I think …   That's right.   ~~What do you think (of …)?~~
> What's your opinion (of …)?   Yes, but …

1 Asking for opinions: _What do you think (of …)?_
   _____

2 Giving opinions: _____
   _____

3 Agreeing: _____
   _____

4 Disagreeing: _____
   _____

Writing — post a website comment

3 Read the text and the comments. Choose the correct options.

> New research shows that people spend four hours online – playing video games, using social media, texting and tweeting – and four hours thirty minutes watching TV. Do we live in a virtual world? Do we talk less to real people? What do you think?
>
> **RS, Wales** I ¹*think /* (*agree*). People don't talk to each other anymore. They work with computers and they ² *too / also* relax with them.
>
> **Agata, Poland** You're ³ *right / agree*. I don't think we live in the real world. We look at computer screens at work, then watch TV in the evening, too. We are ⁴ *too / also* always on our phones. But we don't talk on them – we play with them!
>
> **Paolo, Italy** I don't ⁵ *know / agree* about that. People communicate in different ways! Some people chat online, others chat on their phones. And sometimes we also have conversations with real people ☺. I'm afraid I don't really ⁶ *think / agree* with these opinions.
>
> **Meg, Australia** That's ⁷ *true / agree*, Paolo. What's the problem? For me, computers are fun, but I spend time with friends, ⁸ *too / now*.

I can …	Very well	Quite well	More practice
ask for and give opinions.	○	○	○
agree and disagree.	○	○	○
post a comment on a website.	○	○	○

8 Travel and transport

8.1 I went to ...

Vocabulary holidays

1 Match the phrases in the box to the photos.

> go on a tour   go sightseeing   go swimming
> meet local people   stay in a hotel   trek in the mountains
> visit a museum   visit an art gallery

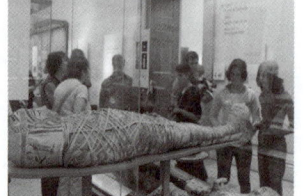

1 _go on a tour_
2 _____
3 _____
4 _____
5 _____
6 _____
7 _____
8 _____

2 Choose the correct word/phrase to complete the text.

My kind of holiday

In the 1970s, travel to other countries was quite expensive and it was more typical to ¹*stay in your own* / *go to another* country for your holiday. My family stayed in Wales. In summer, we drove to Tenby in South Wales for two weeks and we spent every day on the beach. It wasn't always hot, so we didn't ²*trek* / *lie* on the beach – we played beach volleyball with the local kids and we ³*had* / *went* swimming in the sea.

The first time I went to ⁴*another* / *my own* country was on a school trip to Paris. I went ⁵*with a group of friends* / *on my own* from my history class and we had a great time, even with the teachers! We went ⁶*sightseeing* / *a tour* and we ⁷*trekked* / *visited* lots of museums and art galleries.

Now I live in a small village, but I hardly ever ⁸*stay* / *go* in the countryside for my holidays. I like going on ⁹*beach holidays* / *my own* in the summer and on city breaks at other times of the year. Last week I was in Prague. I rented ¹⁰*an apartment* / *a cheap hotel* for a few days and looked ¹¹*at* / *around* the city. I didn't have a map with me and I ¹²*got* / *went* lost once or twice, but I had a good time.

52   Oxford 3000™

Grammar past simple questions

3 Make past simple questions with the words in (brackets). Use the same verb in A and B.

1. **A** I went to Venice last week.
   B (you / on your own)
   Did you go on your own?
2. **A** They visited the National Art Gallery.
   B (they / the Natural History Museum)
   _____
3. **A** She stayed near the centre of town.
   B (she / in an expensive hotel)
   _____
4. **A** We took photos of the sights.
   B (you / photos of the local people)
   _____
5. **A** He bought a sandwich to eat on the beach.
   B (he / a drink)
   _____
6. **A** We had a map of the city.
   B (you / a guidebook)
   _____
7. **A** You passed the English exam.
   B (I / the French exam)
   _____

4 Tick (✓) or correct the questions.

1. Did you went on holiday last year?
   Did you go on holiday last year?
2. Had your parents a good time in Budapest?
   _____
3. Why did Marcus get lost?
   _____
4. How long were you spend in Gambia?
   _____
5. Did she enjoy the tour of the city?
   _____
6. Did they booked the plane tickets online?
   _____
7. Whereabouts in Dubai they stayed?
   _____
8. Who you did go with?
   _____

5a Complete the conversation between Jeff (J) and Anna (A) with the questions from the list.

- Did John go with you?
- Did you have a good time in the USA?
- did you stay in hotels
- How far did you drive?
- what did you do
- what was your favourite place
- ~~When did you get back from your holiday?~~

J Hi, Anna. ¹ _When did you get back from your holiday?_
A Last night. I'm really tired though – it was a long flight back.
J Oh dear. ² _____
A Yes, I did, thanks. I had a fantastic time.
J ³ _____
A No, he didn't, unfortunately. He had to work, so I went with Jenny – she's an old friend from university.
J Oh right. So, ⁴ _____?
A Well, first we flew to Boston, then we rented a car and drove down the coast to Miami.
J Really? ⁵ _____
A It was about 1,300 miles, I think.
J Wow! And ⁶ _____?
A Sometimes, but usually we went to campsites or small guest houses. It was good because we met lots of people that way.
J So, ⁷ _____?
A It's a bit difficult to say because we had a great time everywhere, but my favourite place was probably South Carolina – it was really beautiful and I loved Charleston.

b 8.1))) Listen and check.

PRONUNCIATION did + pronoun in questions

6a 8.2))) Listen and choose the correct option.

1. Where in Morocco did _they / you_ stay?
2. Did _they / he_ take lots of photos in Marrakech?
3. What did _she / you_ think of the local food?
4. Did _I / she_ leave the camera in the hotel?
5. How many nights did _she / we_ spend in Fez?
6. How did _she / he_ travel from Rabat to Casablanca?

b 8.2))) Listen again. Pause the listening and repeat after each question. Pay attention to the pronunciation of _did_ + subject.

I can …	Very well	Quite well	More practice
talk about holidays.	○	○	○
ask questions using the past simple.	○	○	○

8.2 Journeys

Vocabulary transport

1 Match each text 1–4 to two photos a–h.

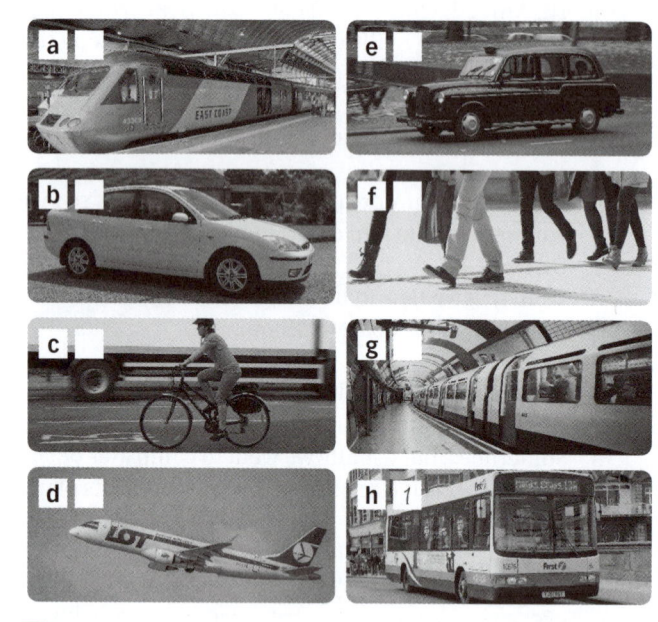

1 Mary
I work in a café in the centre of York, but I live fourteen miles away in Pocklington. There's a bus to York every hour, and when I first moved here I took the bus to work. Last summer I decided to get fit so I bought a bike. Now I cycle every day – it takes about an hour and it saves money.

2 Diana
My parents live in York, but I'm at university in London. I usually go back to York once a month. I take the underground to King's Cross railway station and get the train there. There are regular trains to York – one every half-hour and the journey takes under two hours.

3 Jacob
I don't often use public transport – it's quite expensive and not very comfortable. York is a small city and I prefer to get around the city on foot. I like walking and it helps me to keep fit. If I go out in the evening to a restaurant or to the theatre, I usually take a taxi home.

4 Artur
I'm from Poland and so is my girlfriend, Maggie. We work in York and only go back to Poland once or twice a year. We've got a car, but we don't drive to Poland – we go by plane. There's an airport near York and there are flights to Poland three times a week.

2 Circle the correct answer(s). Sometimes two or more answers are correct.
1 I usually take the ___ to work.
   a (train) b (bus) c public transport
2 Jamie missed his ___ to Paris.
   a underground b plane c train
3 It's an hour from here to the town centre on ___.
   a bike b bus c foot
4 They got a ___ to the station.
   a bike b taxi c car
5 Steve never walks – he goes everywhere by ___.
   a car b bike c public transport
6 Hurry up, we don't want to ___.
   a go by our train b miss the train c get the train
7 You can travel around the city by ___.
   a bus b plane c underground
8 I don't like public transport so I never travel by ___.
   a taxi b bike c train
9 We missed the ___ and arrived late for work.
   a taxi b bus c public transport
10 Do you want to walk to the theatre or ___?
   a go on foot b miss your bus c get the bus

Grammar have to, don't have to, should, shouldn't

3 Put the words in the right order to make sentences.

Hong Kong bus travel

1 follow / the bus company / Passengers / rules / should .
   Passengers should follow the bus company rules.

2 the bus driver / You / to / from / buy / a / have / ticket .
   _____

3 your / You / an old person / offer / seat / should / to .
   _____

4 have / seat / You / to / book / don't / a .
   _____

5 to / You / seat belts / have / the / use .
   _____

6 eat or drink / bus / You / inside / the / shouldn't .
   _____

54 Oxford 3000™

4 Put the sentences from exercise **3** under the right heading.

1 It's the right thing to do – a good idea.
   _____
   _____

2 It's the wrong thing to do – a bad idea.
   _____
   _____

3 It's necessary to do this.
   Passengers should follow the bus company rules.
   _____

4 It's not necessary.
   _____
   _____

5 Choose the correct forms to complete the web page.

PRONUNCIATION *should* and *have to*

6a 8.3))) Listen and circle the correct words.
1 You *should* / *shouldn't* buy a travel card.
2 You *have to* / *don't have to* buy a ticket.
3 You *should* / *shouldn't* wear your seat belt.
4 You *should* / *shouldn't* put your bag there.
5 You *have to* / *don't have to* show your passport.
6 You *should* / *shouldn't* drive when you're tired.
7 You *have to* / *don't have to* pay to visit the museum.
8 You *have to* / *don't have to* come with me.
9 You *should* / *shouldn't* take a map with you.

b 8.3))) Listen again. Pause the listening and repeat after each sentence.

OCTOPUS CARDS

Octopus cards are travel cards which people buy and use to travel on public transport in Hong Kong. You ¹ *have to* / *don't have to* have one to travel around; however, they are very useful. You ² *should* / *shouldn't* think about buying a card when you arrive. They save time because you ³ *shouldn't* / *don't have to* stand in queues or find money to buy single journey tickets.

You can use the cards on all kinds of public transport. You can also use them in some taxis – but you ⁴ *should* / *shouldn't* always ask the taxi driver when you get into the taxi. You ⁵ *should* / *shouldn't* ask at the end of your journey.

You ⁶ *have to* / *don't have to* show your card to anyone when you travel. You just ⁷ *have to* / *should* hold your card near a machine called an Octopus reader at the beginning and end of your journey.

Octopus cards are popular with local people and visitors, and you can buy the cards at any train station. You ⁸ *don't have to* / *shouldn't* lend your card to other people and you ⁹ *should* / *shouldn't* tell the Octopus company if you lose your card.

I can …	Very well	Quite well	More practice
talk about transport.	○	○	○
use *have to/don't have to/should/shouldn't*.	○	○	○

55

8.3 Vocabulary development

Vocabulary expressions with *get*, *take* and *have*

1 Tick (✓) the correct phrases. Put a cross (✗) next to the incorrect phrases.
   1 have
      a a taxi ✗
      b a good time ✓
      c something to eat ✓
   2 get
      a a bus
      b a shower
      c a text message
   3 take
      a a taxi
      b a long time
      c fun
   4 get
      a a sleep
      b emails
      c a taxi
   5 have
      a lunch/dinner
      b a long time
      c a sleep
   6 take
      a a bus
      b photos
      c a text message
   7 have
      a a long time
      b fun
      c a shower

2 Choose the correct option.
   1 We usually have *lunch* / *dinner* at seven o'clock.
   2 There weren't any buses so we took *a long time* / *a taxi* to the station.
   3 Not many people know my mobile phone number so I don't get many *text messages* / *emails*.
   4 We were hungry so we had *a shower* / *something to eat*.
   5 Tanya should have *a sleep* / *fun* if she's tired.
   6 Did you get the *bus* / *email* that I sent you?
   7 We took some great *photos* / *taxis* with our new camera.
   8 The train was very slow and it took a *good time* / *long time* to get to Madrid.
   9 I get a *bus* / *text message* to work every day.

Vocabulary review

3 Complete the different kinds of holiday.

| another country   a beach holiday   a city break |
| the countryside   a group of friends   your family |
| your own   your own country |

   1 going on: *a beach holiday* , _____ , _____
   2 going to: _____
   3 going with: _____ , _____
   4 staying in: _____ , _____

4 Complete the phrases. Use the words in the box.

| around   lie   local   lost   mountains   museums   rent |
| sea   sightseeing   stay   tour |

   1 get *lost*
   2 go on a _____
   3 go _____
   4 go swimming in the _____
   5 _____ on a beach
   6 look _____ the town
   7 meet _____ people
   8 _____ an apartment
   9 _____ in hotels
   10 trek in the _____
   11 visit _____ and art galleries

5 Complete the table with the words in the box. You can use some words more than once.

| bike   bus   car   foot   plane   public transport   taxi |
| train   underground |

go by	go on	miss	take/get
bike		your bus	a taxi
bus		your _____	the bus
		your _____	the _____
			the _____

6 Make expressions using the words in the box. Put them under the correct heading. You can use words more than once.

| a bus   dinner   emails   fun   a good time   a long time |
| lunch   photos   a shower   a sleep   a taxi   a text message |

   1 *get*
      get a bus _____
      _____ _____
   2 *have*
      _____ _____
      _____ _____
      _____ _____
   3 *take*
      take a bus _____
      _____ _____
      _____ _____

56   Oxford 3000™

8.4 Speaking and writing

Speaking — at the train station

1 Use the words to complete the phrases.

| come back | cost | help | next | platform | single | take | ~~travel~~ |

1 When would you like to _travel_ ?
2 When's the _____ train to Perth?
3 How much does a sleeper _____ ?
4 Would you like a _____ or a return?
5 When would you like to _____ ?
6 How long does it _____ ?
7 Which _____ does it leave from?
8 How can I _____ you?

2a Complete the conversation between Adam (A) and a Ticket seller (TS).

> 600 rand … OK. Which platform does the train leave from?
> ~~Hello. I want to get to Cape Town.~~   Just a single, please.
> OK, and how long does it take?   Right. How much is a sleeper ticket?
> Thank you.   Tomorrow, if possible. When's the next train?

TS Good morning. How can I help you?
A 1 _Hello. I want to get to Cape Town._
TS OK. When would you like to travel?
A 2 _____
TS The next one leaves the day after tomorrow, on Tuesday at 13.09.
A 3 _____
TS About twenty-six hours. It arrives at 15.30 on Wednesday.
A 4 _____
TS Would you like a single or a return?
A 5 _____
TS OK, then tourist-class tickets cost 600 rand. There aren't any first-class sleepers on the train.
A 6 _____
TS It goes from that platform over there.
A 7 _____

b 8.4))) Listen and check.

c 8.4))) Listen again. Pause the listening and try to say Adam's part of the conversation. Then listen to check.

Writing — email: a perfect holiday

3 Complete the emails with *so* or *because*.

> Thanks for your email. I'm in Buenos Aires at the moment. It's fantastic! Today I looked around la Boca, where tango dancing started and went on a cycle tour of the sights. It's really interesting ¹_____ I took lots of photos. We decided to stay here another week ²_____ there is so much to see and do.

> We arrived in Machu Picchu in Peru yesterday. I was tired after the journey ³_____ it took five days to walk there. Lucian wasn't very well ⁴_____ we took a bus on the last day. It's amazing to think people built this 6,000 years ago!

4 Match beginnings 1–4 to the endings of the sentences a–d.

1 It was very expensive   ___
2 We ate out a lot   ___
3 The beaches are amazing   ___
4 We got lost   ___

a because we didn't take a map.
b so we went swimming every day.
c so we didn't buy it.
d because the local food was so good.

➡ **STUDY TIP** Use illustrations and photos in your Course book or Workbook to see how well you remember vocabulary from your course. Go back to early units in your Coursebook or Workbook. Look at the pictures in each unit and try to remember the important words or phrases.

I can …	Very well	Quite well	More practice
use expressions with *get*, *take* and *have*.	○	○	○
ask for information at the train station.	○	○	○
write an email about your perfect holiday.	○	○	○

57

8.5 Reading for pleasure

The Silent Brothers

1 Complete the sentences with words from the box. Check any new words in your dictionary.

marry   quarrel   silent   will

  a When two people are in love, they sometimes _____.
  b When someone dies, they leave their money to someone in their _____.
  c You can't hear anything when everything is _____.
  d When people are very angry with each other, they often _____.

2 Look at this picture. Do you think the two men like each other?

3 Read an extract from *The Silent Brothers*, one of the stories in *Stories from the Five Towns* by English author Arnold Bennett. It is about two brothers, John and Robert. They live in the same house but they have not said a single word to each other for ten years. Then their friend, Mr Liversage, brings a letter from their sister Mary, who died three months before.

4 Complete the phrases with the names of characters from the story.

Annie   John   Liversage   Mary

  a _____ had a lot of money.
  b _____ and _____ were in love with Annie.
  c _____ is a business woman.
  d _____ asks _____ not to say anything.
  e _____ thinks the brothers are stupid.
  f _____ knew about the will before the brothers read it.

5a What happens next? Read the sentences and match them to the pictures. Then put them in the right order.
  1 'Mr Hessian!' she cried. ___
  2 'There. That's all.' ___
  3 'I don't want the money, dear,' said Annie. 'They can keep their twelve thousand pounds.' ___

b Answer the questions.
  1 Will Annie marry one of the two brothers? Why (not)?
  2 Who do you think will get Mary's money?
  3 Will the two brothers start speaking to each other again?

You are both very stupid, John and Robert, and I've often said so. Nobody understands why you quarrelled like that about Annie Emery. Your life is difficult, but you've also been very unkind to Annie. She's waited ten years already. So, John, if you marry Annie Emery, I shall give all my money to you. And Robert, if you marry her, I shall give it all to you. And you must be married in twelve months' time. And if neither of you marry her, then I give all my money to Miss Annie Emery, businesswoman, of Duck Bank, Bursley.

Mary Ann Bott, widow

'There. That's all,' Liversage finished.
'Let me see,' said John. Liversage gave him the will and he looked at it carefully.
Robert walked around the table and looked at the paper in his brother's hand.

All three men were silent for a few minutes. Each was afraid to speak, and even afraid to look at the others.
'Well, I must go,' said Liversage, standing up.
'I say,' said Robert. 'You won't say anything about this to Annie, will you?'
'I will say nothing,' agreed Liversage. (But it was wrong of him to say this, because Annie already knew.)
The two brothers sat and thought for a long time.
Ten years before, when Annie was a woman of twenty-three, without family, she started a business for herself, which was a bookshop. John was in love with her, but so was Robert. And the two men quarrelled.

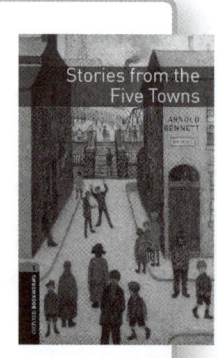

Text extract from *Oxford Bookworms: Stories from the Five Towns*.

58 Oxford 3000™

Review: Units 7 and 8

Grammar

1 Make the sentences negative.
   1 I went on holiday with my friends.
      I didn't go on holiday with my friends.
   2 The train left at half past six.
      _____
   3 They took a taxi to the airport.
      _____
   4 We had an Indian meal last night.
      _____
   5 Sally got lost in Berlin.
      _____
   6 You sent me an email yesterday.
      _____
   7 I read this book last week.
      _____
   8 Sandro and Max flew to Mumbai.
      _____

2 Choose the correct word/phrase to complete the conversation.
   A Where ¹(did you decide)/ you decided to go on holiday?
   B To India. I bought the plane ticket last week.
   A ² *You bought / Did you buy* it online?
   B Yes, I ³ *did buy it / did*. It was cheaper and I ⁴ *didn't have to / shouldn't* go to the British Airways office – it's always busy.
   A How ⁵ *did / were* you pay for it?
   B With my credit card. Now there's just one thing to do – I ⁶ *have to / should* get a new passport. How long does it take to get one?
   A I don't know. You ⁷ *should / shouldn't* phone the passport office.
   B I can do that now. The boss isn't here.
   A Well, do it quickly. You ⁸ *shouldn't / don't have to* use the office phone.

Vocabulary

3 Complete the words in the text.
   Newspaper and magazine articles ¹t e_ l_ l_ us how to be healthy, but some of their ideas are expensive. You don't have to go to the ²g___ to get fit – you can exercise for free. You can do ³y_____ at home or ⁴j____ in the park. Cycling is good for you, too – ⁵b_____ a bike from a friend if you don't have one.
   Doing physical ⁶j_____ round the house is also a great way to use calories.
   Do you know that you can even save money when you exercise? For example, stop taking the ⁷b____ to work, get up early and go on ⁸f_____. You can take ⁹f_____ and vegetables to work for lunch and not spend money on expensive sandwiches. And don't forget to ¹⁰d_____ lots of water – it's free!

4 Complete the information with the verbs in the box. You can use some verbs more than once.

   | go have meet stay take visit |

   Do you want to ¹ *have* fun and learn to salsa? Try a dance holiday in Cuba. You ² _____ in a hotel in Havana and have dance lessons every day. It doesn't ³ _____ a long time to learn your first dance. In the afternoon, there's time to ⁴ _____ sightseeing. You can ⁵ _____ on an island tour, ⁶ _____ a museum or an art gallery – or just ⁷ _____ a taxi to the beach. In the evening you ⁸ _____ dinner with the other students and we take you to a salsa club where you ⁹ _____ local people and dance all night.

Speaking

5 Complete the conversation with the phrases in the boxes.

   | I agree I don't know I think yes, but ~~your opinion~~ |

   A What's ¹ *your opinion* of the new teacher?
   B ² _____ she gives the children too much homework.
   A ³ _____ about that. Schoolwork is important.
   B ⁴ _____ my children don't have any time to do sport. I want them to do well at school and be healthy.
   A ⁵ _____ with you. Maybe we can do some sport at the weekend.

9 Cooking and eating

9.1 Food and drink

Vocabulary food and drink

1 Put the letters in the right order to make the food and drink words in the photos.

1 ardbe _bread_
2 maj _____
3 nhyoe _____
4 yguhotr _____
5 febe _____
6 moroshums _____
7 ecri _____
8 lmenadoe _____
9 daals _____
10 lioevs _____
11 aatsp _____
12 spare _____
13 kiccnhe _____
14 rosecentw _____
15 loonsed _____
16 meolns _____

2 Match the definitions to a word from exercise 1.

1 A small fruit that is black or green. You can eat them or make oil with them to use in salads or to fry food in. _olives_
2 A type of red meat. _____
3 A cold drink you can buy in a shop or café. _____
4 A yellow vegetable. _____
5 You use it to make toast. _____
6 An animal and a type of meat. _____
7 A popular type of food from Italy. _____
8 A type of food made from milk. It often contains fruit. _____
9 It's made from sugar and fruit and you eat it on bread or toast. _____
10 A type of fruit that can be green, yellow or red. _____
11 Small vegetables that are usually brown or white. _____
12 A popular type of food that grows in India and China. _____

Grammar countable and uncountable nouns

3 Are the nouns countable (C) or uncountable (U)?

1 yoghurt _U_
2 a lemon _C_
3 toast ___
4 pears ___
5 food ___
6 honey ___
7 sweetcorn ___
8 pasta ___
9 a vegetable ___
10 olives ___
11 an egg ___
12 bread ___
13 beef ___
14 drinks ___
15 mushrooms ___

60 Oxford 3000™

4 Complete the text with *a/an* or (-).

On a typical working day I'm usually in a hurry and there's only time for ¹ _—_ coffee and ² _____ yoghurt at home. I'm trying to eat more ³ _____ fruit, so I take ⁴ _____ apple or ⁵ _____ pear to eat in the car.

I work in a busy newspaper office and there isn't time for a long lunch. I get ⁶ _____ sandwich and ⁷ _____ bottle of water from the staff canteen and I have them at my desk. I try not to eat between meals, but people often bring ⁸ _____ cakes to work when it's their birthday, so sometimes I have ⁹ _____ cake and ¹⁰ _____ cup of coffee.

Dinner is my main meal of the day. That's usually something like ¹¹ _____ chicken with ¹² _____ salad or ¹³ _____ vegetables. I don't eat after dinner, but I do occasionally have ¹⁴ _____ glass of milk before I go to bed because I think it helps me to sleep.

5 Complete the conversation between Elizabeth (E) and the Assistant (A) with *some* or *any*.

E Hi, two chicken sandwiches on brown bread, please.
A Sorry, we don't have ¹ _any_ chicken today.
E Do you have ² _____ beef?
A Let me check … Yes, there's ³ _____ beef. What would you like with it?
E I'd like ⁴ _____ salad, please. But please don't put ⁵ _____ tomatoes or onions in the sandwiches.
A Anything else?
E Yes, can I have ⁶ _____ mushroom soup?
A Of course. And would you like ⁷ _____ drinks?
E Two bottles of Coke, please.
A I'm sorry, we haven't got ⁸ _____ Coke – just water or lemonade.
E Two bottles of lemonade then.

6 Put the words in the right order to make sentences. Each sentence has one extra word that you don't need.
1 like / I'd / please / some / sandwich, / a .
   I'd like a sandwich, please.
2 some / there / Are / noodles / any ?
   _____
3 an / don't / eggs / We / any / have .
   _____
4 bottles of water / some / They / a / need .
   _____
5 yesterday / Mark / any / made / cakes / some .
   _____
6 there / Is / pasta / a / any ?
   _____
7 didn't / I / some / this morning / have / breakfast / any .
   _____

PRONUNCIATION weak sounds in *some* and *any*

7a 9.1))) Listen and put the sentences in each group in order (1–4).
1 a ___ Is there any rice in the cupboard?
  b _1_ There isn't any rice in the cupboard.
  c ___ Can I have some rice from the cupboard?
  d ___ There's some rice in the cupboard.
2 a ___ Is there any milk in the fridge?
  b ___ There isn't any milk in the fridge.
  c ___ Can I have some milk from the fridge?
  d _1_ There's some milk in the fridge.

b 9.1))) Listen again. Pause the listening and repeat after each sentence.

I can …	Very well	Quite well	More practice
talk about food and drink.	○	○	○
use countable/uncountable nouns with *some/any*.	○	○	○

61

9.2 In the kitchen

Grammar *much/many* and quantifiers

1 Make present simple questions with *how much/how many*.
1 time / you / spend cooking
   How much time do you spend cooking?
2 fruit / you / eat
   _____
3 eggs / you / buy each week
   _____
4 fruit juice / you / drink
   _____
5 times a week / you / have takeaway food
   _____
6 calories / be / there in a pizza
   _____
7 salt / you / put on your food
   _____
8 milk / be / there in the fridge
   _____

2 Order the amounts from small to big.

| a lot of   ~~none~~   not many   not much   quite a lot of   some |

1 *none*
2 _____ / _____
3 _____
4 _____
5 _____

3 Choose the correct answer to each question.
1 A How much fruit do you buy each week?
   B Oh, we buy *a lot* / *a lot of* fruit every week.
2 A How many eggs are there in the cupboard?
   B *None* / *Not much* – I forgot to buy them.
3 A How many potatoes do we need for the soup?
   B *Not many* / *Not a lot of* – just three or four.
4 A How much money do you spend in the supermarket?
   B We spend quite *a lot* / *much* – food is very expensive.
5 A How many recipe books do you have?
   B *Some* / *A lot of*, but not many – I don't like cooking.
6 A How much salt did you put in this soup?
   B *Not many* / *Not much*. I never use *a lot* / *a lot of* salt.

4 Choose the correct word or phrase to complete the article.

How ¹*many* / *much* money does it cost to stay healthy?

Food prices today mean that ² *some* / *much* people in the UK are finding it difficult to buy food. The British Heart Foundation (BHF) wants people in the UK to be healthy. They asked 2,444 people about the food they bought, and they found that ³ *quite a lot of them* / *none* (42%) didn't have the money they needed to eat healthily.

Doctors say that people need to eat ⁴ *not many* / *a lot of* fruit and vegetables every day to stay healthy. The BHF spoke to adults who earn under £10,000 to find out ⁵ *how many* / *how much* of them eat fruit and vegetables regularly. The answer is ⁶ *a lot of them* / *not many*, because fresh fruit and vegetables are expensive.

Good food is important for good health and the BHF has ⁷ *some* / *not many* ideas for people who don't have ⁸ *much* / *some* money to spend on food, or for people who just want to eat well and save money. There's a meal plan to show how two people can eat healthily for under £50 a week.

You don't have to be a great cook – there are ⁹ *lot of* / *a lot of* simple recipes on the website to try. ¹⁰ *A lot of* / *None* the recipes use expensive ingredients and they don't take ¹¹ *much* / *many* time to make. You can visit the BHF website and see people trying ¹² *some* / *none* of the recipes in their own homes.

62   Oxford 3000™

Vocabulary in the kitchen

5 Match items (a–h) in the illustration to words 1–11. Put a cross (✗) next to the three things which aren't in the illustration.

1. a bowl _c_
2. a food-processor ___
3. a fork ___
4. a frying pan ___
5. a kettle ___
6. a knife ___
7. a microwave ___
8. an oven ___
9. a plate ___
10. a saucepan ___
11. a spoon ___

6 Circle the correct word: a, b or c.
1. Chop the vegetables with a sharp ___.
   a oven   b (knife)   c bowl
2. Here's a ___ to eat your soup.
   a spoon   b fork   c kettle
3. Put the food on the ___ and take them to the table.
   a saucepans   b kettles   c plates
4. Boil some water in the ___.
   a kettle   b frying pan   c food-processor
5. Where are the ___ for the soup?
   a plates   b forks   c bowls
6. Food cooks very quickly in a ___.
   a kettle   b microwave   c spoon
7. Put the vegetables in the ___ and mix them.
   a food-processor   b microwave   c oven
8. You eat with a knife and ___.
   a bowl   b fork   c plate
9. Fry the eggs in that frying ___.
   a oven   b bowl   c pan

➡ **STUDY TIP** Make labels to put on items around your home/office. Write the name of the item in English. Each time you see the item, look at the label and practise saying the word. This is a good way to help you remember the names of things that you see or use every day.

7 Circle the incorrect phrase.
1. roast potatoes   roast chicken   (roast jam)
2. chop carrots   chop rice   chop onions
3. fry lemonade   fry mushrooms   fry eggs
4. bake pies   bake yoghurt   bake cakes
5. mix food in a bowl   mix food in a food-processor   mix food in a fork
6. boil water   boil butter   boil milk

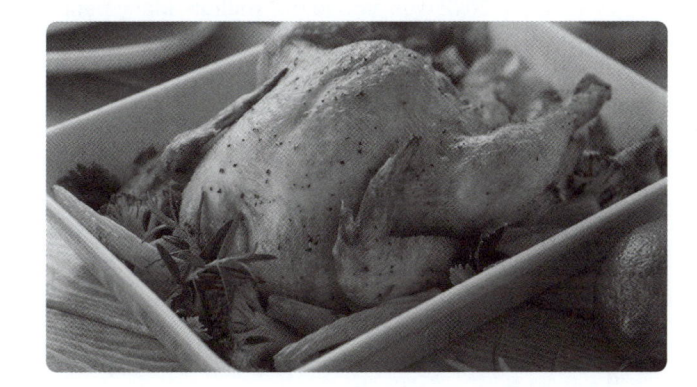

I can …	Very well	Quite well	More practice
talk about cooking.	○	○	○
talk about quantifiers.	○	○	○

9.3 Vocabulary development

Vocabulary say numbers

1a Write the numbers and dates next to the words.
1. five million — 5,000,000
2. three quarters _____
3. the fourteenth of July _____
4. nineteen sixty-seven _____
5. three point nine _____
6. eighteen per cent _____
7. seventy-three degrees Celsius _____

b 9.2))) Listen and repeat the numbers and dates.

2a Look at the facts and figures about Brazil. Write how we say the numbers and dates in **bold**.

Facts and figures about Brazil

Brazil is the world's ᵃ**5th** largest country. It covers nearly a ᵇ**½** of South America, and the coast of Brazil is ᶜ**7,491 km** long! More than ᵈ**200,000,000** people live in Brazil and ᵉ**87%** of them live in towns and cities. The capital city is Brasília, which is home to around ᶠ**2,700,000** people. Brazil's main language is Portuguese, but Brazil became an independent country in ᵍ**1822**. People celebrate Independence Day on ʰ**6ᵗʰ September**, which is a national holiday.

Brazil is a popular place for foreign tourists. According to the World Tourism Organization, the number of visitors in ⁱ**2012** was around ʲ**5.7 million**. Many people go to Rio de Janeiro on the east coast. One of Rio's most famous sights is the statue, Cristo Redentor, which is ᵏ**30 m** high, at the top of the Corcovado mountain. You can walk to the statue, but be careful in summer when Rio's average temperature is between 25°C and ˡ**30°C**!

a _fifth_   g _____
b _____   h _____
c _____   i _____
d _____   j _____
e _____   k _____
f _____   l _____

b 9.3))) Listen and say the numbers and dates from the text.

Vocabulary review

3 Complete the food words by adding the missing letter.
1. _b_ eef
2. b__ead
3. ch__cken
4. hon__y
5. ja__
6. bottle of lemona__e
7. __emons
8. m__shrooms
9. noodl__s
10. oli__es
11. pas__a
12. p__ars
13. ric__
14. sal__d
15. swe__tcorn
16. yoghur__

4 Write the words in the correct column.

bake boil ~~bowls~~ chop food-processor fork fry
frying pan kettle knife microwave mix oven plates
roast saucepan spoon

Kitchen equipment and utensils	Cooking verbs
bowls	

5 Put the numbers with the correct heading.

billion a fifth forty metres a half million
minus ten degrees Celsius nine point seven
nought/zero degrees a quarter six centimetres a third
thirty-two per cent thousand ~~the twelfth of May~~

1. date: _the twelfth of May_
2. decimal: _____
3. fraction: _____, _____, _____, _____
4. height and length: _____, _____
5. large numbers: _____, _____, _____
6. percentage: _____
7. temperature: _____, _____

Oxford 3000™

9.4 Speaking and writing

Speaking in a restaurant

1 **9.4** Listen to the conversation in a restaurant. Circle the correct answers.
   1 They're in an *Italian / Chinese / Mexican* restaurant.
   2 They are having *breakfast / lunch / dinner* in the restaurant.
   3 Jack orders *fish / salad / soup* for his starter.
   4 Anna orders *salad / pasta / fish* for her main course.
   5 They order *a starter and a main course / a starter and a dessert / a main course and a dessert*.
   6 Jack orders *one / two / three* side dishes with his main course.
   7 They drink *fruit juice / coffee / water* with their meal.

2a **9.5** Listen and complete the questions from the restaurant.
   1 _Would you like_ to order lunch now?
   2 _____ a starter?
   3 _____ have the soup of the day, please?
   4 _____ have a mixed salad, please?
   5 _____ have the pasta with mushroom sauce?
   6 _____ any side dishes with that?
   7 _____ have some rice and some steamed vegetables?
   8 _____ something to drink?
   9 _____ have a bottle of water, please?

b **9.5** Listen again and repeat the questions.

Writing asking about and recommending a place to eat

3a Choose the correct options.

> Hi Julia,
> How are you? Everything's good with me. I'm going to Bath on Sunday with James. I know you lived there and I ¹*hope / want* you can help me with something. It's James's birthday and ²*I'm looking / I look* for a nice restaurant to have lunch. What's your ³*favourite / best* restaurant? James loves Indian food. Do you know ⁴*anywhere / anyone* with good Indian food? Also, where is ⁵*a good place / anywhere* to eat with a nice view? Are the restaurants in Bath busy on Sundays? Do I ⁶*need / should* to book a table?
> Thanks for your help!
> Harriet

b Put Julia's answers in the right order to answer Harriet's questions.

> Hi Harriet
> a ___ It's an upstairs room in a beautiful old building with a nice view.
> b ___ OK, have a brilliant time and let me know how it goes!
> c _1_ Great to hear from you and I'm glad to hear you're well.
> d ___ The waiters are really friendly, too, so I think you should go there.
> e ___ My favourite place is the Hole in the Wall because the food is amazing, but it's quite expensive.
> f ___ There's a wonderful Indian restaurant called the Eastern Eye.
> g ___ It's popular, but you don't usually need to book because it has a lot of tables.
> Julia

I can …	Very well	Quite well	More practice
ask about and recommend a place to eat.	○	○	○
order food in a restaurant.	○	○	○

10 The world around us

10.1 The weather

Vocabulary the weather

1 Match the weather words in the box to photos a–c.

cloudy dry ~~foggy~~ freezing icy rainy
snowy sunny warm wet windy

a

foggy _____ _____ _____

b

c

2 Complete the sentences with a verb from the box.

blew froze ~~rained~~ shone snowed

1 The ground was wet after it _rained_ during the night.
2 The high winds _____ down one of the trees in my garden.
3 They went skiing after it _____ .
4 We had a great day at the beach – the sun _____ all day.
5 The rainwater _____ and turned to ice.

3 Look at the UK weather map and circle the best words to complete the weather forecast.

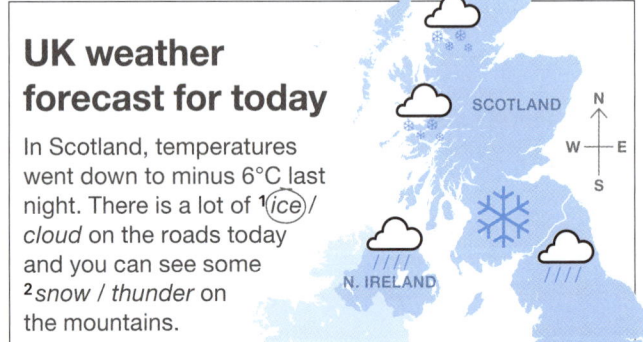

UK weather forecast for today

In Scotland, temperatures went down to minus 6°C last night. There is a lot of ¹(ice)/ cloud on the roads today and you can see some ²snow / thunder on the mountains.

Northern Ireland and the north of England is going to have more ³ice / rain.

In Wales, it's a good idea to stay indoors today because there's a very big ⁴storm / fog with lots of thunder and lightning and very high ⁵winds / rain.

The east of England is dry, but it is difficult to see in some places because there is heavy ⁶sun / fog.

There are some ⁷clouds / rain in the south of England, but it is warm and sunny and there is more ⁸sun / lightning to come later.

66 | Oxford 3000™

Grammar comparative adjectives

4a Write the comparative form of these adjectives.
1 low — *lower*
2 big — _____
3 early — _____
4 bad — _____
5 interesting — _____
6 expensive — _____
7 tall — _____
8 late — _____
9 dry — _____
10 fat — _____

5 Complete the text about the weather in different parts of Pakistan with the comparative form of the verb in (brackets).

FACTS ABOUT PAKISTAN

Some of the highest mountains in the world are in northern Pakistan. It is much ¹ *higher* (high) and ² _____ (cold) there than the rest of the country during the winter. The capital city, Islamabad, is in the north-east. Winter and spring in Islamabad are ³ _____ (cool) than summer and autumn. Summer is from May to September. These months are ⁴ _____ (hot) and ⁵ _____ (sunny) than the other months of the year. The second half of summer is the rainy season, so it is ⁶ _____ (wet) than the first half.

Karachi is Pakistan's largest city. It is on the southern coast. Like Islamabad, Karachi is very hot in summer, but it has ⁷ _____ (low) rainfall than Islamabad. It's probably ⁸ _____ (good) to visit Karachi in winter or spring than in summer because the temperatures are ⁹ _____ (comfortable).

6 Tick (✓) or correct the sentences.

1 New York is old than Sydney.
   New York is older than Sydney.
2 Is life in the city more expensive than life in the country?
   _____
3 The weather is more bad today than it was yesterday.
   _____
4 My new job is interesting than my old job.
   _____
5 I think spring and autumn are nicer summer or winter.
   _____
6 Karachi is more big than Islamabad.
   _____
7 Is French easier to learn than German?
   _____

PRONUNCIATION than in comparative sentences

7a 10.1))) Read and listen to the sentences. Does *than* have a weak sound /ðən/ (W), or a strong sound /ðan/ (S)?
1 This hotel is more expensive than that hotel. *W*
2 China is bigger than Thailand. ___
3 Winter is colder than summer. ___
4 I think surfing is better than skiing. ___
5 Travelling by train is more interesting than flying. ___
6 Some people are friendlier than others. ___

b 10.1))) Listen again and repeat. Copy the pronunciation.

I can ...	Very well	Quite well	More practice
describe the weather.	○	○	○
use comparative adjectives.	○	○	○

10.2 Natural wonders

Vocabulary nature and geography

1 Look at the photos and complete the grid. What is number 9?

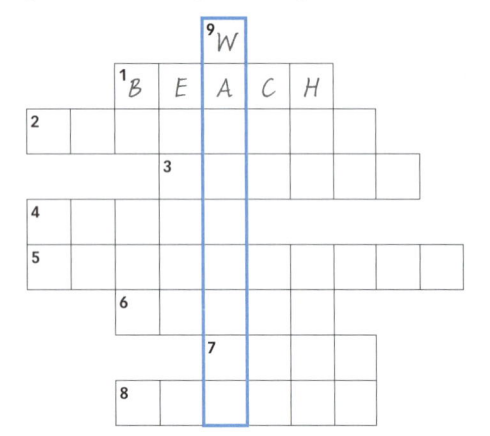

⁹W
¹B E A C H

2 Choose the correct words to complete the text.

Hawaii

Hawaii is a group of ¹*islands* / *deserts* in the middle of the Pacific Ocean. The biggest ² *island* / *mountain* in the group is Hawai'i (also called The Big One) but the state capital, Honolulu, is on the south ³ *rainforest* / *coast* of the third largest island, O'ahu.

Things to do and see in Hawaii

- Go for a walk in the Ka'ū ⁴ *Desert* / *Lake* (take plenty of water with you as it's very hot and dry there).
- Spend a day lying on the world famous ⁵ *waterfall* / *beach* in Waikiki or learn to surf there.
- Trek through the beautiful Hawaiian ⁶ *lake* / *rainforest*. Wear good walking boots and take a camera to photograph the birds and animals that live there.
- Visit Mauna Kea – the highest ⁷ *mountain* / *beach* in Hawaii. You can drive to the top of Mauna Kea in about two hours and near the top you can visit ⁸ *Lake* / *Coast* Waiau – but don't go into the water or drink it.
- Relax on a boat trip along the Wailua ⁹ *Mountain* / *River*.
- Take a trip to the Waimea Falls Park on O'ahu. There you can swim in the pool underneath the fifteen-metre high ¹⁰ *waterfall* / *mountain*.

3 Label the compass with words from the box.

| east | ~~north~~ | north-east | north-west | south |
| south-east | south-west | west | | |

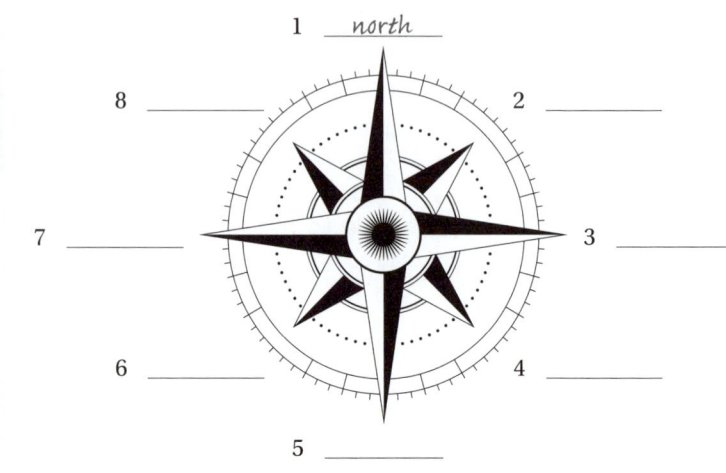

1 _north_

68 | Oxford 3000™

Grammar: superlatives

4 Complete the travel tips with the superlative form of the adjectives in (brackets).

Getting to Oʻahu

Honolulu International Airport is Hawaii's
¹ _largest_ (large) and ² _____ (busy) airport. Most visitors arrive here.

Getting around

One of the ³ _____ (good) ways to get around the capital, Honolulu, is by public transport, but the ⁴ _____ (easy) way to see the rest of the island is by car.

When to visit

Any time of year is a good time to visit the island, but the ⁵ _____ (warm) and ⁶ _____ (dry) part of the year is between April and November.

The beaches

The ⁷ _____ (famous) beaches on Oʻahu are Waikiki and North Shore. North Shore is the ⁸ _____ (popular) beach for surfing.

Accommodation

The ⁹ _____ (big) hotels are in Waikiki, but the hostels and campsites are probably the ¹⁰ _____ (cheap) places to stay.

5 Make sentences and questions with superlatives.
1. the Congo River / deep / river in the world
   (+) _The Congo River is the deepest river in the world._
2. summer / usually / hot / time of the year
   (+) _____
3. what / old / city in the world
   (?) _____
4. Mount Kilimanjaro / high / mountain in Africa
   (?) _____
5. which / interesting / museum in Rome
   (?) _____
6. that / bad / hotel in the town
   (+) _____
7. yesterday / sunny / day of the week
   (+) _____

6 Choose the best way to complete the sentences.
1. It was *colder than* / *the coldest* day of the year.
2. The Himalayas are *higher than* / *the highest* the Alps.
3. Prague is one of *more beautiful* / *the most beautiful* cities in Europe.
4. Are the Petronas Towers *taller than* / *the tallest* buildings in Malaysia?
5. The weather is *worse* / *the worst* now than it was last week.
6. Where are *the windier* / *the windiest* places in the world?

PRONUNCIATION: superlatives

7a 10.2))) Listen and match the phrases and the photos.

the best   the dirtiest   ~~the fastest~~   the hottest
the most dangerous   the oldest

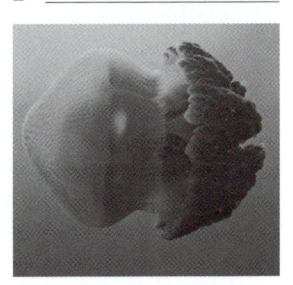

1 _the fastest_   4 _____
2 _____   5 _____
3 _____   6 _____

b 10.2))) Listen again and repeat.

I can …	Very well	Quite well	More practice
describe nature and geography.	○	○	○
use superlative adjectives.	○	○	○

10.3 Vocabulary development

Vocabulary collocations

1 Choose the correct options to complete the collocations.
 1 India got a high (score)/ number in the hockey match and won the game.
 2 The *high / deep* price of houses in the UK makes it difficult for young people to buy their first home.
 3 We arrived late because there was *heavy / strong* traffic on the motorway.
 4 I'm a very *mild / light* sleeper. Any small noise wakes me up.
 5 It was a very *bad / freezing* storm – all of the buses and trains stopped running.
 6 Australia has very *weak / mild* winters – the average temperature is 15°C.

2 Underline the incorrect collocation in each group.
 1 a deep sleeper   a deep lake   a deep mountain
 2 a mild storm   a mild day   mild weather
 3 strong winds   a strong accent   a strong sleeper
 4 a hard worker   a hard coffee   a hard job
 5 a close friend   a close relative a close person
 6 high traffic   high prices   a high salary

3 Choose a noun to go with each pair of opposite adjectives.

| coffee sleepers temperatures traffic ~~winds~~ |

 1 strong/light _winds_
 2 deep/light _____
 3 high/low _____
 4 heavy/light _____
 5 weak/strong _____

Vocabulary review

4 Put the words under the correct heading.

| ~~to blow~~ ~~cloud~~ ~~cloudy~~ dry fog foggy to freeze freezing ice icy lightning rain to rain rainy to shine snow to snow snowy storm sun sunny thunder warm wet wind windy |

 1 weather adjectives
   cloudy, _____

 2 weather nouns
   cloud, _____

 3 weather verbs
   to blow, _____

5 Match the words in the box to the definitions.

| beach coast desert island lake mountain rainforest river ~~waterfall~~ |

 1 A place where water moves from a high place to a low place.   _waterfall_
 2 A large hot and dry area with a lot of sand, e.g. the Sahara. _____
 3 An area of sand next to the sea. _____
 4 A very large hill, e.g. Everest. _____
 5 A large area of land with lots of trees and plants where it rains a lot. _____
 6 A large area of water with land all around it, e.g. Baikal. _____
 7 A long area of water that travels across land to a sea or a lake, e.g. the Nile. _____
 8 The land that is next to the sea. You often find beaches here. _____
 9 An area of land with water all around it, e.g. Cuba. _____

6 Put the letters in the right order to find the compass points.
 1 stea _east_   3 utosh _____
 2 hontr _____   4 stew   _____

7 Complete the collocations with words from the box.

| accent coffee friend prices sleeper ~~storm~~ traffic weather worker |

 1 bad   _storm_
 2 close _____
 3 deep   _____
 4 hard   _____
 5 heavy _____
 6 high   score / salary / temperature / _____
 7 light _____
 8 mild   _____
 9 strong coffee / winds / _____
 10 weak _____

70 Oxford 3000

10.4 Speaking and writing

Speaking reasons and preferences

1 Match the words from the box to the photos.

> ~~compass~~ cooking equipment first aid kit GPS lighter
> map sleeping bag stove tent torch

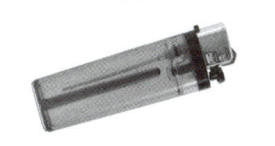

1 _compass_
2 _____
3 _____
4 _____
5 _____
6 _____
7 _____
8 _____
9 _____
10 _____

2 Correct the sentences about a camping trip.
1 I think we should to take a torch.
   I think we should take a torch.
2 I'm prefer to take a first aid kit instead of a stove.
   _____
3 The most usefulest things to take are the sleeping bags.
   _____
4 A map is more important a lighter.
   _____
5 Use a stove is a better idea than make a fire.
   _____

3a Read the sentences in exercise 2 again and choose the best reason.
1 ... because *it rains at night* / *(it's dark at night)*.
2 ... because *we can use wood to make a fire* / *we could get tired*.
3 ... because *it's cold at night* / *they're expensive*.
4 ... because *it's difficult to sleep in the forest* / *it's easy to get lost*.
5 ... because *it's difficult to make a fire in the rain* / *a stove is heavy to carry*.

b 10.3))) Listen to the sentences, and say the reason. Then listen and check.

→ **STUDY TIP** Record yourself when you practise a speaking activity. Listen to the recording and check your pronunciation.

Writing describe places

4 Match the two halves of the sentences about Uganda.

> ### Come to Uganda!
> 1 We have many rivers and lakes including Lake Victoria, _b_
> 2 You can fish, and take boat trips to visit the ___
> 3 Uganda also has some of the best national parks ___
> 4 Temperatures in Uganda are more comfortable than ___
> 5 It is usually wet, but there are two dry seasons. It is nicer to ___
> 6 Ugandans are friendly and welcoming and the country is one of ___
>
> a in the world, where you can see a lot of wonderful birds and animals.
> b the world's largest tropical lake.
> c the most beautiful in Africa. Come and visit!
> d visit between December and February, and June and August.
> e islands and see many different birds and animals.
> f many tropical areas because of the height of the country.

I can ...	Very well	Quite well	More practice
use adjective + noun collocations.	○	○	○
give preferences and reasons.	○	○	○
write a description of a place.	○	○	○

10.5 Listening for pleasure

A TV cookery programme

1a Match the words in the box to the definitions.

> ingredients   recipes   utensils

1 the instructions that you use to cook different meals
   _____
2 the different types of food that you need to make a meal
   _____
3 the equipment that you use to cook a meal
   _____

b Decide if the following are parts of a recipe (R), ingredients (I) or utensils (U). Check the meaning of any new words in your dictionary.

1 boil ___   5 garlic ___
2 saucepan ___ 6 herbs ___
3 roast ___   7 wash ___
4 knife ___   8 grill ___

2 Match the ingredients and verbs in the box to the photos.

> to boil   garlic   to grill   herbs   olive oil   to wash

1 *to boil*   4 _____
2 _____   5 _____
3 _____   6 _____

3 10.5))) Listen to an extract from a TV cookery programme.

4a Match the questions and answers from the cookery programme.

1 How are you? *g*
2 What are you cooking for us today? ___
3 Is the recipe difficult? ___
4 Does it take a long time to prepare? ___
5 What ingredients are you using? ___
6 Do you want me to help? ___
7 Is this one of your own recipes, Marcus? ___

a No, this is one of my mother's.
b Well, for the milk chicken, you need a chicken, half a litre of milk, ...
c ... I'm doing my own special milk chicken with lemon roasted potatoes.
d Yes, please. I need you to wash the chicken first.
e No, not long.
f No, it isn't – it's very simple.
g Fine thanks, Steve.

b 10.5))) Listen again and check.

5a 10.6))) Listen and read the questions from the cookery programme. Does the speaker's voice go up or down at the end of the question? Circle the correct answer.

1 How are you?   up (down)
2 What are you cooking for us today?   up   down
3 Is the recipe difficult?   up   down
4 Does it take a long time to prepare?   up   down
5 What ingredients are you using?   up   down
6 Do you want me to help?   up   down
7 Is this one of your own recipes, Marcus? up   down

b Complete the sentences.

1 The speaker's voice goes *up / down* at the end of *yes/no* questions that begin with *do* and *be*.
2 The speaker's voice goes *up / down* at the end of questions that begin with a question word.

72

Review: Units 9 and 10

Grammar

1 Choose the correct options.

A Hi, I'd like **¹**(some)/ *much* chicken, please. About 250 grams.
B Sure. Anything else?
A Yes, **²** *a* / *-* bottle of olive oil and **³** *any* / *some* black olives.
B Here you are.
A Er, do you have **⁴** *much* / *any* mangoes?
B Yes, we've got **⁵** *quite a lot* / *many* of mangoes. How **⁶** *many* / *much* do you want?
A Just three. And can I have some **⁷** *lemon* / *lemons*?
B I'm sorry, we don't have **⁸** *any* / *some* today.

2 Complete the text with the comparative or superlative form of the adjective in (brackets).

Mount Everest

Mount Everest is the **¹** _highest_ (high) mountain in the world. It is also one of the **²** _____ (difficult) mountains to climb. Climbers have to practise on **³** _____ (small) mountains before they try to climb Everest and they have to be very fit. Only the **⁴** _____ (fit) people get to the top!

Climbers need quite a lot of money, too. Everest is one of the **⁵** _____ (expensive) mountains to climb because you need special equipment and guides. There are lots of **⁶** _____ (cheap) places to go climbing!

There are often very strong winds in the mountains and it is **⁷** _____ (dangerous) to climb when it is windy. The **⁸** _____ (good) time of the year to climb Everest is in the spring when it is **⁹** _____ (safe) and there is more chance of success than at other times. Summer is the **¹⁰** _____ (bad) time to climb because of the weather.

Vocabulary

3 Match the definitions to five of the words in the box.

> bake   chop   a food-processor   a fork   a frying pan
> honey   a kettle   a lemon   mix   a plate   roast
> a saucepan   a spoon   toast

1 You mix different foods in it. _____
2 You cook food in it. _____
3 You eat soup with it. _____
4 Cook meat in the oven. _____
5 Cut into smaller pieces. _____

4 Complete the text with the words/phrases from the box.

> coast   high winds   hot   ~~island~~   mild weather   mountain
> 1.2 million   rain   temperatures   a tenth

Mauritius is a small **¹** _island_ in the Indian Ocean with a population of **²** _____. Over **³** _____ of the population (150,000 people) live in the capital city, Port Louis. Mauritius is two thousand miles from Southeast Africa. It has beautiful sandy beaches – the best ones are on the east **⁴** _____. The highest part of Mauritius is Pieter Both, an 823-metre high **⁵** _____ in the centre of the island.

The weather in Mauritius doesn't change very much. Summer is from November to April and the weather can be quite **⁶** _____. This is also the wettest time of year, with 900 mm to 1,500 mm of **⁷** _____. There are sometimes storms with very **⁸** _____. The country has **⁹** _____ in winter when the **¹⁰** _____ are between 17°C and 23°C.

Speaking

5 Complete the restaurant conversation between Jo (J), Lyn (L) and the waiter (W) with words/phrases from the box.

> can I   course   have   instead   like   ~~the menu~~   to order
> prefer   should

J Can we see **¹** _the menu_, please?
W Certainly. Here you are.
L I think we **²** _____ order quickly because there's a meeting at 2.30.
J OK. Er ... excuse me?
W Would you like **³** _____ now?
J Yes. Could I **⁴** _____ the tomato soup and a cheese salad, please?
W Of **⁵** _____. And for you, madam?
L **⁶** _____ have a mushroom omelette, please?
W Would you **⁷** _____ something to drink?
J A small bottle of lemonade for me. Lyn?
L The same, please. Oh, sorry, no. I think I'd **⁸** _____ to have a bottle of sparkling water **⁹** _____.

73

11 Working together

11.1 Community spirit

Vocabulary verb + noun collocations

1 Match the collocations to the photos.

give a present to someone
help someone with their homework
teach someone to drive   visit someone in hospital

1  _____   3 _____

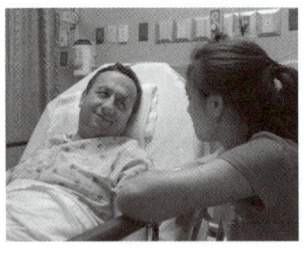

2  _____   4 _____

2 Look at the sentences. Find the verb + noun collocation.

1 It isn't always easy to look after a child on your own.
  look after a child
2 We should plant a tree in the garden.
  _____
3 Shall I make some sandwiches for the picnic?
  _____
4 Does Joe know how to repair a bike?
  _____
5 How can we improve the town?
  _____
6 It took three days to paint the room.
  _____
7 Mark wants to organize a party for his parents.
  _____

3 Complete the collocations in the text with verbs from the box.

give   help   improve   look after   make   organize   plant
repair   teach   visit

THE BEST WAY TO HELP!

It's easy to ¹ _give_ money to charity, but why not think about doing something good for others? In Catherine Ryan Hyde's book, *Pay It Forward*, the main character is Trevor, a boy with an idea to ² _____ the world by helping people. He thinks that when someone does a good thing for you, you shouldn't do a good thing for them. Instead, you should 'pay it forward' and do a good thing for three more people.

The story shows us how to make changes with little things. So how can you 'pay a good thing forward'?

Why not:

- ³ _____ someone with their shopping?
- ⁴ _____ an elderly neighbour and talk to them?
- ⁵ _____ a neighbour's dog and take it for a walk?
- ⁶ _____ a cake to sell for charity?
- ⁷ _____ an event for people in your area, like a party or a sports day?
- ⁸ _____ someone to read?
- ⁹ _____ broken furniture and give it to someone who needs it?
- ¹⁰ _____ some flowers in your area?

74 | Oxford 3000™

Grammar *going to* for plans and intentions

4 Complete the sentences with the correct form of *going to*. Use the verb in (brackets).
1. We *'re going to organize* a basketball competition. (organize)
2. Some of the students _____ a game. (play)
3. We _____ tickets to the event. (not sell)
4. I _____ people to give money to charity. (ask)
5. You _____ time to watch the competition. (not have)
6. You and Tony _____ sandwiches and drinks to sell. (make)
7. Ahmed _____ a poster. (design)
8. Sandy _____ – she's on holiday. (not help)
9. I _____ this again – it's too much work! (not do)

5 Make questions with *going to*.
1. what time / the party / start
   What time is the party going to start?
2. what / you / wear for your interview
   _____
3. Andy / meet / us at the airport
   _____
4. what colour / we / paint / the bathroom
   _____
5. your children / go / to university
   _____
6. how / Alice / travel / to Nairobi
   _____
7. you / learn Arabic / when you move to Bahrain
   _____
8. Maria / buy / the cinema tickets online
   _____

6 Write the questions from exercise **5** with the correct answers.
1. A *What time is the party going to start?*
   B The invitation says half past nine.
2. A _____
   B Yes, I am.
3. A _____
   B Well, I like blue and white.
4. A _____
   B I think she's going to take the train.
5. A _____
   B No, they aren't. They're going to look for jobs.
6. A _____
   B No, he isn't. We have to get a taxi to the hotel.
7. A _____
   B Yes, she is. She's going to pay for them with her credit card.
8. A _____
   B I'm going to buy a new dress tomorrow.

PRONUNCIATION *going to*

7a 11.1 Read and listen to the sentences. Is *to* a strong sound /tuː/, or a weak sound /tə/?
1. What are you going to do?
2. I'm going to visit my grandparents tomorrow.
3. Is Annie going to drive to Berlin?
4. We aren't going to have a holiday this year.
5. Liam is going to cook dinner for us.
6. Ella isn't going to come to the theatre with us.

b 11.1 Listen again. Pause the listening and repeat after each sentence.

8a 11.2 Listen to these negative sentences. Which part of the verb do we stress in each sentence?
1. I'm not going to go out.
2. He isn't going to call you.
3. We aren't going to buy it.
4. They aren't going to come.
5. You aren't going to have much time.
6. She isn't going to make dinner.

b 11.2 Listen again. Pause the listening and repeat after each sentence.

I can …	Very well	Quite well	More practice
use *going to* for plans and intentions.	○	○	○
use verb + noun collocations.	○	○	○

11.2 Challenges

Vocabulary technology

1a Complete the crossword.

```
¹W  E  B  ²S  I  T  E
          |
         ³|  |  |  |
          |
         ⁴|  |  |
     ⁵|  |
     |
     |
     ⁶|  |  |  |
```

Across ▶
1 A place on the internet where you can find information about a subject.
3 Small computer programmes for a mobile phone or a tablet.
4 Short for Global Positioning System.
6 A small computer – you use it by touching the screen.

Down ▼
2 A mobile phone that can make phone calls and connect to the internet.
5 A short piece of writing sent from one mobile phone to another.

b 11.3))) Listen, check and repeat.

2 Complete the paragraphs with words from exercise **1a**. There is one word you do not need.

TECHNOLOGY FIRSTS

1 The first _website_ was at CERN – the European Organization for Nuclear Research. Its address is http://info.cern.ch/hypertext/WWW/TheProject.html.

2 The 1992 IBM Simon Personal Communicator was the first _____. It was 20 cm long and weighed 0.5 kg. You could make phone calls with a Simon and send and receive emails.

3 In 1992, Neil Papwell, a 22-year-old engineer, sent the first _____. It read 'Merry Christmas'.

4 Nowadays, many people use a _____ instead of maps when they're travelling. The American government developed it in the 1970s, but you couldn't buy it until the 1980s.

5 Computer companies designed the first _____ in the 20th century, but they didn't really become popular until after 2007. This was when technology improved so mobile computers could do more and were easier to use.

3a Write how you say the website and email addresses. Use words from the box.

| at dash dot forward slash underscore |

1 www.nelsonmandela.org
   www dot nelson mandela dot org

2 anton@russorest.com
   anton at russorest dot com

3 www.bbc.co.uk/news
   _____

4 joel_kubi@mailbox.com
   _____

5 www.whitehouse.gov/
   _____

6 mark-derby@mailbox.au
   _____

b 11.4))) Listen and check.

c 11.4))) Listen again. Pause the listening and repeat after each address.

➡ **STUDY TIP** Try to find time to go back and review language regularly and to add new things you have learnt to your notebook. You can also use the Vocabulary reviews in each unit to revise what you have learnt in lessons and to see how much you remember.

76 Oxford 3000™

Grammar: infinitive of purpose

4 Complete the text using the infinitive form of verbs from the box.

explain find look ~~organize~~ read sell show teach

My smartphone

I always carry my smartphone with me and I use it ¹ _to organize_ my life. I work for a software company that designs apps ² _____ to universities. The universities buy them ³ _____ their online courses. This means I have to go to a lot of meetings, so I use my smartphone as a diary – it tells me where I need to be at different times of the day. And when I visit universities ⁴ _____ people our new software apps, the GPS app on my smartphone shows me how to get there. If I am going to arrive somewhere late, I can call ⁵ _____. Sometimes I travel to Europe or North America and I take my smartphone with me ⁶ _____ at travel websites and ⁷ _____ information about flights and hotels, and also ⁸ _____ emails from my office. My father says it's just an expensive phone, but I say it's my personal assistant!

5 Match questions 1–8 to answers a–h.

1. Why do you play tennis?
2. Why do they shop online?
3. Why are they going to the market?
4. Why did you phone me?
5. Why did she join the army?
6. Why is he going to the airport?
7. Why are you learning Chinese?
8. Why are we stopping here?

a To meet his sister.
b To get a job in China.
c To save time and money.
d To help her country.
e To buy fruit.
f To keep fit.
g To buy more petrol.
h To tell you about my holiday.

6 Complete the sentences and questions with the verbs in (brackets). Use the correct form of *going to* for one verb and the infinitive of purpose for the other.

1. We _'re going to leave_ home at 7 a.m. tomorrow _to take_ the train to Istanbul. (leave / take)
2. He _____ a part-time job _____ some money. (get / earn)
3. _____ you _____ a new suit _____ for your interview? (buy / wear)
4. The presidents of the two countries _____ next week _____ the future. (meet / talk about)
5. I _____ my brother _____ me his car tomorrow. (ask / lend)
6. She _____ my laptop _____ an email to the university. (use / write)
7. We _____ some sandwiches _____ with us to the beach. (make / take)

I can …	Very well	Quite well	More practice
talk about technology.	○	○	○
say why I do things/use the infinitive of purpose.	○	○	○

11.3 Vocabulary development

Vocabulary making adjectives stronger

1 Write the strong adjectives in the correct place.

awful beautiful brilliant excellent fantastic freezing lovely terrible wonderful

1 very nice: _beautiful_, _____
2 very good: _____, _____, _____, _____
3 very bad: _____, _____
4 very cold: _____

2 Replace the normal adjectives in **bold** with a strong adjective from the box.

crucial delighted great huge tiny

On 21st July 1969, over 500 million people watched American astronauts land on the moon. The two men who left their spaceship to walk on the moon looked ¹ **very small**, but this was a ² **very big** event in the history of space travel. Everyone at NASA was ³ **very happy**. The moon landing wasn't just a ⁴ **very good** result for the astronauts, but for all of the people who worked at NASA and who were ⁵ **very important** to the success of the moon landing.

1 _tiny_   4 _____
2 _____   5 _____
3 _____

3 Rewrite the sentences with *very*. If *very* isn't possible, use *really*.

1 Janine is a nice person.
   Janine is a very nice person.
2 His exam results were brilliant.
   His exam results were really brilliant.
3 Our neighbours are unfriendly.
   _____
4 Your dog is noisy.
   _____
5 The singer was terrible.
   _____
6 We made a huge cake for John's birthday.
   _____
7 The letter wasn't important.
   _____

Vocabulary review

4 Complete the verb + noun collocations.

help improve look after make organize plant repair teach (x2) visit

1 _help_ someone with something, e.g. their homework
2 _____ somewhere, e.g. your area or your workplace
3 _____ someone or something, e.g. a pet or a child
4 _____ something for someone, e.g. a cake
5 _____ something, e.g. an event
6 _____ something, e.g. a tree
7 _____ something, e.g. a bike, broken furniture
8 _____ someone something, e.g. a language
9 _____ someone to do something, e.g. to drive
10 _____ someone, e.g. a neighbour, someone in hospital

5 Complete the sentences.

an app a GPS a smartphone a tablet a text websites

1 _A GPS_ helps you to find a place and not get lost.
2 You can make phone calls and go online with _____.
3 _____ is a small programme you can download on to a smartphone or a computer.
4 There are millions of _____ on the internet where you can find information out about almost anything.
5 _____ is a message that you write and send from one mobile phone to another.
6 _____ is a small mobile computer.

6 Write the words next to the symbols.

at dash dot forward slash underscore

1 @   _at_   4 .   _____
2 _   _____   5 -   _____
3 /   _____

Oxford 3000™

11.4 Speaking and writing

Speaking — offering to do something

1 Put the words in the right order to make offers.
1. I / a text / send / Shall / him ?
   Shall I send him a text?
2. I / a lift / you / Why / don't / give ?
   _____
3. help / you / I'll / for / to look / them .
   _____
4. help / Let / you / me / it / with .
   _____
5. like / me / to show / you / Would / you ?
   _____
6. Shall / phone / for / I / a pizza ?
   _____

2 Match these situations to the offers from exercise **1**.
1. I forgot to tell Patric about the meeting.
   Shall I send him a text?
2. I can't find the key to the games cupboard.
   _____
3. I need to get to the youth club before seven.
   _____
4. I don't know how to use this printer.
   _____
5. I'm too tired to cook tonight.
   _____
6. This box of sports equipment is very heavy.
   _____

3a Complete the conversation about the youth club trip with the offers from the list.
- Shall I make a drink?
- ~~Shall I write that down?~~
- Let me help you.
- I'll email the design to you when it's ready.
- Why don't I do that?
- Would you like me to print the posters?

A This is the list of the things for the youth club trip to the coast.
B OK, this looks fine, but we'll need some sports equipment, too, so we can play football and volleyball on the beach.
  ¹ _Shall I write that down?_
A Good idea. Use my pen. Right, let's go through the list. First, we'll need to organize a bus to take everyone there.
C ² _____
  I've got more time than you and I can phone the bus company this afternoon.
A Perfect. Now what about a poster to tell everyone about the trip? I can write the text, but I'm not very good at art.
C ³ _____
  We can design the poster together on my new tablet.
A Thanks, Carlos.
B ⁴ _____
  I can use the printer at the university.
A OK. ⁵ _____
  Now, what's next?
C It looks like it's going to be a long evening.
  ⁶ _____
B Oh, I'd love a coffee.

b 11.5 🔊 Listen and check.

Writing — a notice

4a Read the lines from two notices. Which are formal (F) and which informal (I)?
1. Come to Room 5 on Friday at 1 p.m.! _I_
2. Would you like to live close to the university with a friendly group of people? ___
3. Join the office chess club. ___
4. We are looking for a fourth person to share a student house. ___
5. If you are interested, call Naomi Brandon on 08952 727445. ___
6. Want to do something different at lunchtimes and make new friends? ___
7. Wanted: chess players ___
8. Do you need a cheap room to rent for next year? ___

b Put the lines in the two notices in a suitable order.

I can …	Very well	Quite well	More practice
make adjectives stronger.	○	○	○
offer to do something.	○	○	○
write a formal/informal notice.	○	○	○

12 Culture and the arts

12.1 Artistic ability

Grammar present perfect simple

1 Complete the article with the present perfect simple form of one of the verbs in (brackets).

ANDREA BOCELLI

Italian singer Andrea Bocelli is rich and successful, but some times in his life ¹ _haven't been_ (not be / not sing) easy. Andrea had an accident when he was twelve and he is blind, but this ² _____ (not make / not stop) his dream of singing. Andrea ³ _____ (do / sell) over 100 million records and he ⁴ _____ (become / be) world famous. He ⁵ _____ (watch / travel) to lots of different countries to give concerts and thousands of people ⁶ _____ (give / watch) him sing, including Pope John Paul II.

The people in Andrea's home town, Lajatico, ⁷ _____ (build / do) an outdoor theatre – Teatro del Silenzio. It only opens one day a year, when Andrea sings there. Some of his famous friends ⁸ _____ (visit / sing) there with him; they include the Spanish opera singer Plácido Domingo. Andrea is famous as an opera singer, but he ⁹ _____ (not record / not buy) only classical music. Canadian pop star Celine Dion ¹⁰ _____ (become / make) a record with Andrea, and so has Italian rock star Zucchero.

2 Make questions using the present perfect form of the verbs in (brackets). Then complete the short answers.
  1 _Have_ you _heard_ (hear) Andrea Bocelli's songs?
    Yes, I _have_ .
  2 _____ he _____ (record) any songs in your language?
    No, he _____ .
  3 _____ he _____ (give) concerts in your country?
    Yes, he _____ .
  4 _____ you _____ (go) to one of his concerts?
    No, I _____ .
  5 _____ your friends _____ (buy) any of his records?
    Yes, they _____ .
  6 _____ you and your husband _____ (visit) Lajatico?
    No, we _____ .

3 Correct the present perfect simple sentences.
  1 We're visited Moscow and St Petersburg.
    We've visited Moscow and St Petersburg.
  2 You read this book?
    _____
  3 We hadn't a holiday.
    _____
  4 All of the workers have went home.
    _____
  5 Mandy isn't found a job.
    _____
  6 Who has took my bike?
    _____
  7 I hasn't heard the weather forecast.
    _____
  8 He did washed the car.
    _____

80 Oxford 3000™

PRONUNCIATION sentence stress

4 **12.1** Listen to sentences 1–6. Then tick (✓) the correct sentence in each pair (1 and 2) below.
1 We haven't seen Jane.
2 She's won a prize.
3 He hasn't been to university.
4 They haven't finished work.
5 You've fixed my computer.
6 I've joined a gym.

1 a In positive sentences the past participle has a stressed sound.
   b In positive sentences the past participle doesn't have a stressed sound.
2 a *Hasn't* and *haven't* have a stressed sound in negative sentences.
   b *Hasn't* and *haven't* don't have a stressed sound in negative sentences.

5 **12.1** Listen to sentences 1–6 again, pause and repeat.

Vocabulary verb and noun phrases

6 Match the words and phrases in the box to the photos.

| an art gallery   a cinema   a classical music concert |
| a dance lesson   a film/movie   an instrument |
| a painting lesson   a play   a salsa class |

1 _a cinema_   2 _____   3 _____
4 _____   5 _____   6 _____
7 _____   8 _____   9 _____

7 Complete the phrases with *go*, *have*, *play* or *see*.

In 1973, Pierre Vellas, a French university professor, started courses for older people to learn new things. He called it the U3A (University of the Third Age) and it is now an international organization. Here is a sample of things you can do with a U3A group:

Art: ¹ _Have_ drawing and painting lessons or ² _____ to an art gallery.

Dance: ³ _____ dance lessons, and then ⁴ _____ to a salsa class and show everyone what you've learned!

Films: Don't ⁵ _____ to the cinema alone – join a U3A film group and ⁶ _____ a new film, then discuss it with your group.

Music: Learn to ⁷ _____ an instrument in a music group. Good musicians can ⁸ _____ in a U3A band.

Theatre: Some groups organize theatre trips to ⁹ _____ a play or a musical.

8a Choose the correct word.
1 A Have you *seen* / *gone* the new *Star Wars* film?
   B Yes, I *saw* / *went* to the cinema with Alex to see it.
2 A Do you want to *have* / *go* to the theatre next week? The new Andrew Lloyd Webber musical is on.
   B That sounds great. I *saw* / *played* his last musical and I loved it.
3 A I'd love to learn to *play* / *have* the guitar like you.
   B Really? I can teach you if you want.
4 A Where's Ping? I haven't seen her today.
   B She's *gone* / *seen* to a rock concert in Berlin.
5 A That's a lovely picture. How did you learn to draw like that?
   B Thanks. I *went* / *had* some drawing lessons last summer.
6 A I really want to go to the Glastonbury festival this year, but I can't get a ticket.
   B I bought my ticket last month – I love *seeing* / *going* to music festivals. My cousin's *playing* / *having* in a band there this year.

b **12.2** Listen and check.

I can …	Very well	Quite well	More practice
talk about past experience and events using the present perfect simple.	○	○	○
use verb and noun phrases.	○	○	○

81

12.2 At the movies

Vocabulary films

1 Complete the film types. Write the missing vowels.

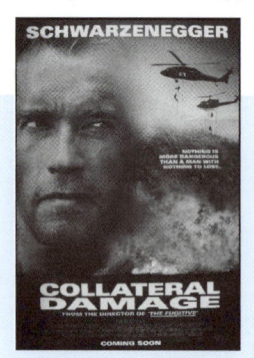

1 _a_ ct _i_ _o_ n films
2 r__m__nc__ films 
3 __n__m__t__ __ns 
4 h__rr__r films 
5 c__m__d__ __s 
6 m__s__c__ls 
7 dr__m__s 
8 sc__ __nc__ f__ct__ __n films 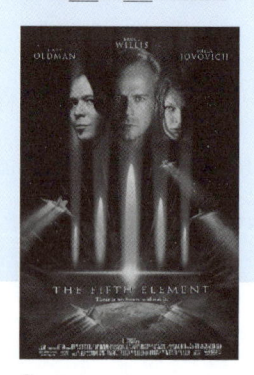

2 Match the definitions to the film types from exercise 1.
1 These films are exciting. You often see people in fights, or driving fast cars. _action films_
2 These films are usually very scary. _____
3 There are spaceships in these films and they are set on other planets. They are often about the future. _____
4 These films don't have real actors. They are usually made with computers. _____
5 These films tell the story of events in people's lives. Sometimes they are sad. _____
6 You laugh at the things that the actors say and do in these films. _____
7 The actors sing and dance in these films. _____
8 These films tell a love story. _____

3 Complete the review with the words in the box.

| about | ~~favourite~~ | it's | set | stars |

A favourite film

One of my [1] _favourite_ films is a Lebanese film called *Caramel*. It is [2]_____ in modern-day Beirut and it is [3]_____ the lives of five Lebanese women. Most of the story takes place in a hairdresser's shop. Some parts of the film are very funny, but *Caramel* isn't a comedy – [4]_____ a drama. It [5]_____ Nadine Labaki and Yasmine Al Masri. Nadine didn't only act in the film, she also wrote the story with Rodney El Haddad and Jihad Hojeily, and she directed the film.

➡ **STUDY TIP** Read the 'can do' statements at the end of each lesson and test yourself to see how much you remember from your course. Try to think of one or two sentences for each grammar 'can do' statement, and five or six words for each vocabulary statement. This will help you to find what areas you need to practise.

Oxford 3000™

Grammar: present perfect simple and past simple

4 Make present perfect simple sentences and add *ever* or *never*.
1 I / have / acting lessons.
   I've never had acting lessons.
2 you / walk / out of a play before the end?
   _____
3 we / go / to a film festival.
   _____
4 you / meet / a famous person?
   _____
5 anyone in your family / be / on TV?
   _____
6 Nadia / sing / in public before.
   _____
7 I / forget / to send you a birthday card?
   _____

5a Complete the pairs of sentences using the verb in **bold**. Use the present perfect simple for one sentence and the past simple for the other sentence.

1 **play**
   A I _'ve_ never _played_ a musical instrument.
   B I _played_ the violin when I was at school, but I wasn't very good.
2 **go**
   A We _went_ to the opera last night. It was great.
   B Really? I _'ve_ never _been_ to the opera. It's not my kind of music.
3 **read**
   A I _____ Paulo Coelho's latest book at the weekend, but I didn't really enjoy it.
   B _____ you _____ any of his other books?
4 **star**
   A Which actor _____ in *The Artist*?
   B That was Jean Dujardin. He's very famous in France – he _____ in a lot of French films.
5 **have**
   A You dance really well. _____ you _____ dance lessons?
   B Yes, we _____ salsa lessons when we went to Cuba last summer.
6 **see**
   A I _____ this film before.
   B When _____ you _____ it?

6 Tick (✓) the correct sentences. Put a cross (✗) next to the incorrect sentences.
1 George has found a new job last week. ✗
2 I've run in two marathons. ✓
3 My parents haven't visited Asia.
4 Everyone has enjoyed the meal last night.
5 She's learned to swim when she was a child.
6 We have stood up and clapped at the end of the play.
7 Have you been here before?

7 Choose the correct options.

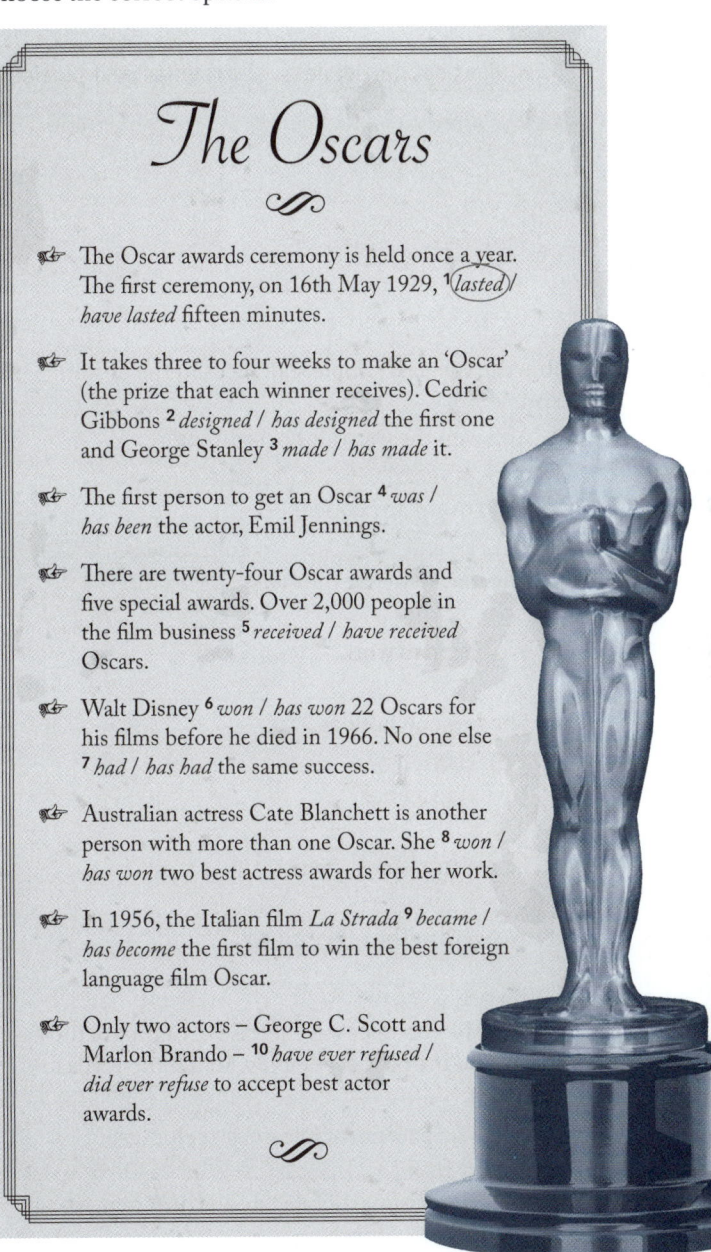

The Oscars

☞ The Oscar awards ceremony is held once a year. The first ceremony, on 16th May 1929, **¹ (lasted)** / *have lasted* fifteen minutes.

☞ It takes three to four weeks to make an 'Oscar' (the prize that each winner receives). Cedric Gibbons **² designed** / *has designed* the first one and George Stanley **³ made** / *has made* it.

☞ The first person to get an Oscar **⁴ was** / *has been* the actor, Emil Jennings.

☞ There are twenty-four Oscar awards and five special awards. Over 2,000 people in the film business **⁵ received** / *have received* Oscars.

☞ Walt Disney **⁶ won** / *has won* 22 Oscars for his films before he died in 1966. No one else **⁷ had** / *has had* the same success.

☞ Australian actress Cate Blanchett is another person with more than one Oscar. She **⁸ won** / *has won* two best actress awards for her work.

☞ In 1956, the Italian film *La Strada* **⁹ became** / *has become* the first film to win the best foreign language film Oscar.

☞ Only two actors – George C. Scott and Marlon Brando – **¹⁰ have ever refused** / *did ever refuse* to accept best actor awards.

I can …	Very well	Quite well	More practice
talk about films.	○	○	○
use the present perfect simple and the past simple.	○	○	○

12.3 Vocabulary development

Vocabulary past participles

1 Write the verb and its past participle in the correct column.

~~act~~ ~~become~~ cry find have like lose play stop think

Regular past participles	Irregular past participles
act – acted	become – became

2 Rewrite the past simple sentences in the present perfect simple.
1 You won the Oscar for best director.
   You've won the Oscar for best director.
2 Who drank my coffee?
   _____
3 She met someone online.
   _____
4 We began to work.
   _____
5 She went on holiday.
   _____
6 He wrote a book.
   _____
7 I gave Tom some money.
   _____
8 We were in the office all day.
   _____

3 Look at the sentences in exercise 2. Compare the past forms and the past participles. Match the verbs to the rules.
   Rule A The past participle doesn't change:
      won/won _____
   Rule B The past participle has one different vowel:
      drunk/drank _____
   Rule C The past participle has an extra syllable:
      _____ _____
   Rule D The past simple and the past participle are completely different:
      _____

Vocabulary review

4 Complete the table with the verbs.

go have play see

1 ___	2 ___	3 ___	4 ___
to the cinema/theatre to a music festival to a salsa class to a classical music concert to art galleries	a film a musical a play	music lessons dance lessons drawing lessons	the guitar a musical instrument in a band

5 Translate the words into your own language.
1 action films _____
2 animations _____
3 comedies _____
4 dramas _____
5 horror films _____
6 musicals _____
7 romance films _____
8 science fiction films _____

6 Complete the table.

Verb	Past simple	Past participle
be	was/were	1 _been_
begin	2 ___	begun
break	broke	3 ___
drink	4 ___	drunk
drive	drove	5 ___
eat	6 ___	eaten
give	gave	7 ___
go	8 ___	been/gone
grow	grew	9 ___
hear	10 ___	heard
wake	woke	11 ___
win	12 ___	won

Oxford 3000™

12.4 Speaking and writing

Speaking on the phone

1a Choose the correct options.
1. Hi, Artem, *it's* / *I am* Megan. *Is* / *It's* Ellie there?
2. Could you ask him to *call back me* / *call me back*, please?
3. She's not here at the *time* / *moment*.
4. *Speak* / *Hang* on a minute. I'll *just* / *soon* get her.
5. *Can* / *Do* you tell her to *call* / *answer* me back, please?
6. I'm *afraid* / *scared* he's *out of* / *into* the office.
7. Could I *have* / *give* your number, please?
8. Hello. *I could* / *Could I* speak to the manager, please?
9. I'm afraid he's unable to *give* / *take* your call at the moment.
10. Hold *on* / *it*.

b 12.3)) Listen, check and repeat.

2 Are the sentences in exercise 1a formal (F) or informal (I)?
1. _I_   3. __   5. __   7. __   9. __
2. _F_   4. __   6. __   8. __   10. __

3a Put the sentences in the right order in each conversation.
a __ B Hi, Chris. Have you booked the restaurant for Alison's surprise birthday party?
   __ B Hi, Alison, it's Bashir. Is Chris there?
   __ B OK. Can you tell him to call me back, please?
   _8_ C No, I haven't had time. I'll do it now and I'll call you back in a minute.
   __ C Hi, Bashir.
   __ A Sorry, he's not here at the moment.
   _1_ A Hello.
   __ A Sure – oh hold on, he's just come back. Chris, Bashir wants to speak to you.

b __ A I'm afraid she's unable to take your call at the moment. Can I help?
   __ A Yes, of course. Could I have your name and telephone number, please?
   __ A Oh, you'll need to speak to the restaurant manager about that.
   _1_ A Good afternoon. How can I help you?
   _8_ B Yes, it's Chris Brown and the number is 072 …
   __ B Maybe. I'd like to book a table for twelve for tomorrow night.
   __ B Could you ask her to call me back, please?
   __ B Hello. Could I speak to the restaurant manager, please?

b 12.4)) Listen and check.

Writing a review

4a Put the words in order to make sentences.
1. about / was excited / seeing / the film, / better / I / but the book / was .
   I was excited about seeing the film, but the book was better.
2. doesn't / the show / like / was / My son / museums, / he thought / usually / amazing / but .
   _____
3. the film / I / to be / expected / but / great, / it / wasn't .
   _____
4. and / the play / thought / was / too long / the main actor / I / terrible / was .
   _____
5. don't / playing / tonight, / again / I / recommend / but / going / They're .
   _____
6. the concert, / enjoyed / a bit / was / I / too loud / but / the guitar player .
   _____
7. the circus / I / was / expect / didn't / good, / to be / amazing / but / it .
   _____
8. recommend / I / thought / fantastic / it / was / and / it / to everyone / I .
   _____

b Decide if the reviews are positive (+) or negative (−). Which sentence is both positive and negative?

I can …	Very well	Quite well	More practice
use past participles.	○	○	○
speak on the phone.	○	○	○
write a review.	○	○	○

85

12.5 Reading for pleasure

An extract from Les Misérables

1 Match the words in the box to the illustrations. Check any new words in your dictionary.

| a bishop   a candlestick   a fire   a plate   a prison |
| a prisoner |

1 _____
2 _____ 
3 _____ 
4 _____ 
5 _____  
6 _____ 

2 Read an extract from *Les Misérables*, a novel by the French writer Victor Hugo. The novel is set in France at a time when life is very hard for poor people.

> 'Come in,' said the bishop. The bishop was a kind man; everyone in the town of Digne knew that. Poor people, hungry people, miserable people – they all came to the door of the bishop's house. 
>
> The bishop's sister looked at the man at the door that night, and she was afraid.
>
> 'Look at him!' she whispered to the bishop. 'He is a big man and a dangerous one. He carries a yellow card, so he was once a prisoner – a bad man.'
>
> But the bishop did not listen. 'Come in, my friend,' he said to the man at the door. 'Come in. You must eat dinner with us, and sleep in a warm bed tonight.'
>
> The man stared at the bishop. 'My name is Jean Valjean,' he said. 'I was a prisoner in Toulon for nineteen years. Here is my yellow card, see? People everywhere shut their doors in my face – but not you. Why not?'
>
> 'Because, my friend, in the eyes of God you are my brother,' said the bishop, smiling. 'So, come in, and sit down by our fire.' The bishop turned to his sister. 'Now, sister, our friend Jean Valjean needs a good dinner. Bring out the silver dinner plates. It's a special night tonight.'
>
> 'Not the silver plates!' whispered the bishop's sister. Her eyes went quickly to Jean Valjean, then back to the bishop's face.
>
> 'Yes, the silver plates,' said the bishop. 'And the silver candlesticks, too.'

Text extract from *Oxford Bookworms: Les Misérables.*

3 Complete the text with one word in each space.

| afraid   bishop's   candlesticks   dinner   kind   open |
| ~~prison~~   sister |

Valjean leaves the ¹ _prison_ in Toulon and goes to a town called Digne. He arrives at the ² _____ house. People don't usually ³ _____ their doors when Valjean arrives at their house, but the bishop is different. He is a ⁴ _____ person and he helps lots of people. The bishop lives with his ⁵ _____. She is ⁶ _____ of Valjean, but the bishop invites Valjean to have ⁷ _____ with them. He tells his sister to use the silver plates and ⁸ _____ for their dinner.

86   Oxford 3000™

Review: Units 11 and 12

Grammar

1 Correct the sentences.
 1 They're going to organizing a charity race.
  They're going to organize a charity race.
 2 I'm saving money for buy a new bicycle.
  _____
 3 He's ever used a GPS before.
  _____
 4 Is your mum going teach you to drive?
  _____
 5 We've been to a concert last night.
  _____
 6 Have you ever ate Peruvian food?
  _____
 7 We're going to go to the hospital visit Kim.
  _____
 8 You aren't having a lot of time tomorrow.
  _____

2 Complete the sentences with the correct form of the verb in (brackets). Use the correct form of *going to*, the past simple, the present perfect simple or an infinitive of purpose.
 A What ¹ _are_ you and Mel _going to do_ (do) for the hospital charity day next week?
 B Mel is organizing a collection ² _____ (buy) new hospital equipment, but I ³ _____ (not have) any good ideas. What about you?
 A Phil and I ⁴ _____ (make) some cakes. We ⁵ _____ (sell) them to hospital visitors. We ⁶ _____ (buy) all the ingredients last night.
 B ⁷ _____ Phil ever _____ (make) a cake before?
 A No, he hasn't, but he ⁸ _____ (borrow) a recipe book from the library yesterday to practise.
 B Right, well, I'm going to call Mel ⁹ _____ (see) if she needs help with the collection.

Vocabulary

3 Choose the correct options.
 1 I'm looking (after)/ with my neighbour's cats this week.
 2 You should plant some flowers in your *garden* / *garage*.
 3 Did you *do* / *make* these sandwiches?
 4 Janet's husband *plays* / *sings* the guitar in a band.
 5 Do you want to see this *film* / *cinema*? I've heard it's very good.
 6 We went to the *theatre* / *play* last week.

4 Choose one word from each pair to complete the text.

a science-fiction film/an animation   app/text
awful/excellent   comedies/dramas   forget/forgotten
freezing/delighted   ~~go~~/been   tablet/GPS   very/really

I haven't ¹ _been_ to the cinema for a long time. The last time was a couple of years ago and I've ² _____ the name of the film and the main actor. It was ³ _____ about a group of people living in space, and it was ⁴ _____ – one of the worst films I've seen! I saw it just before Christmas. It was minus 10°C outside and the cinema was ⁵ _____. The only thing I liked was the big screen – it was ⁶ _____ huge. However, I prefer to watch films at home on my ⁷ _____ computer. I downloaded a film ⁸ _____ a few months ago and now I can watch all the latest films. ⁹ _____ are my favourite – I like funny films.

Speaking

5 Complete the missing words.
 1 A These books are really heavy.
  B S_hall_ I carry them f_____ you?
 2 A W_____ you like me to get you a drink?
  B Yes, please. I'd love a cup of tea.
 3 A Could I h_____ your number, please?
  B Yes, it's 01745 3 …
 4 A Hello. C_____ I speak to the manager, please?
  B I'm afraid he's unable to take your call at the moment.
 5 A Can you ask Mark to call me b_____?
  B Yes, of course.
 6 A I haven't got enough time to finish this report.
  B Why d_____ I help you with it?
 7 A Hi, Yasmine, it's Sara. Is Mum there?
  B H_____ on. I'll just get her.
 8 A I need to get to the railway station.
  B L_____ me give you a lift.

87

Audioscripts

Unit 1 Your world

Page 4, Exercises 1b & c

1.1
1 the USA, American
2 Mexico, Mexican
3 Britain, British
4 France, French
5 Italy, Italian
6 Greece, Greek
7 Poland, Polish
8 Turkey, Turkish
9 the UAE, Emerati
10 Pakistan, Pakistani
11 China, Chinese
12 Vietnam, Vietnamese

Page 4, Exercises 3b & c

1.2
French
Greek
English
Spanish
Turkish
Polish
Urdu
Chinese
Arabic
Italian
Vietnamese

Page 5, Exercise 7b

1.3
J What's your name?
A Amelie.
J That's a French name. Are you French?
A No, I'm not French.
J What's your nationality?
A I'm from Quebec, in Canada - the main language in Quebec isn't English, it's French, so I'm French-Canadian.
J Where is your home?
A My home is in Montreal – it's a big city in Quebec.
J Are your neighbours French-Canadian?
A No, they aren't French-Canadian. My neighbours are from the USA.
J Are you married?
A Yes, I am. My husband's a teacher at the university.
J Are you a teacher?
A No, I'm not a teacher. I'm a doctor at the hospital.

Page 6, Exercise 1b

1.4
1 I   my
2 you   your
3 he   his
4 she   her
5 it   its
6 we   our
7 they their

Page 7, Exercise 9b

1.5
1 My wife and I are from Egypt. Our first language is Arabic.
2 Our neighbours are very nice. They're from India. Their names are Sanjay and Mira.
3 Jean-Paul is from France. He's a restaurant owner. His wife, Annie, is a teacher.
4 Hi. You're the new student. What's your name?
5 Angela's parents are doctors. Angela's a doctor, too.

Page 7, Exercises 10a & b

1.6
1 They're Greek. Their car is German.
2 Henry's at home. Henry's wife is at work.
3 We are late. Our train is at 9 o'clock.
4 He's married. His wife's name is Eleanor.
5 You're late. Where's your homework?

Page 9, Exercise 1

1.7
R Good morning. Can I help you?
J Yes, please. I'm here for the Arabic class.
R OK. Well I need a few details to complete the enrolment form. What's your name?
J Jackie Alamilla.
R How do you spell your surname?
J Alamilla is A-L-A-M-I-double L-A
R And what's your nationality?
J I'm Australian. I'm from Sydney, but I live here in England now.
R OK. Are you a student?
J No, I work.
R What's your job?
J I'm a French teacher.
R Oh, right. OK, last question. What's your email address?
J It's jackie1@alamilla.co.uk
R Sorry, can you repeat that please?
J Yes, it's jackie1@alamilla.co.uk
R Thanks. Right well your course is in classroom 7. That's on the first floor…

Page 9, Exercise 2b

1.8
1 What's your name?
2 How do you spell your surname?
3 What's your nationality?
4 What's your job?
5 What's your email address?
6 Sorry, can you repeat your first name, please?

Unit 2 My day

Page 10, Exercises 3a & b

2.1
1 Lisa loves her job as a herpetologist.
2 Jacob drives to work every day.
3 Yvonne studies English in the evenings.
4 Miyuki teaches maths at the university.
5 My husband works in a lab.
6 Sven relaxes after work.
7 Sally sometimes writes emails to her sister.

Page 10, Exercise 3c

2.2
works
writes
loves
drives
studies
teaches
relaxes

Page 12, Exercises 3a & b

2.3
1 I get up at ten to seven.
2 I go to work at twenty-five past eight.
3 The shop opens at quarter to nine.
4 I have coffee at twenty past ten.
5 I finish work at quarter past four.
6 I arrive home at half past five.

88

7   We usually have dinner at half past seven.
8   I never go to bed before twelve o'clock.

Page 15, Exercise 2b

2.4

Would you like to go out for dinner tonight?

Are you free tomorrow?

What time do you want to eat?

Let's meet at the train station.

Do you want to try that new restaurant near the park?

Where shall we meet?

Yes, that sounds nice.

Yes, I'd love to.

I'm sorry, but I'm busy this evening.

Thanks, but I'm afraid I have plans tonight.

Page 15, Exercise 3b

2.5

A Would you like to go out for dinner tonight?
B I'm sorry, but I'm busy this evening.
A Are you free tomorrow?
B Yes, I am.
A Do you want to try that new restaurant near the park?
B Yes, I'd love to.
A What time do you want to eat?
B Well, I usually have dinner at around eight o'clock.
A OK, let's meet at quarter to eight. Where shall we meet?
B Let's meet at the train station.
A OK. See you tomorrow at the train station.

Page 16, Exercise 3a

2.6

Presenter Our next topic is adult learning. It's autumn now and many adult education classes are starting. Did you know that there are over 5,700 classes at schools and colleges here in Ireland? There are lots of different courses to choose from – you can learn to write a book, play the guitar, or speak a foreign language. Today we want you to tell other listeners about your courses.
Presenter OK, let's talk to caller one, Jade from Clonee near Dublin. Hello, Jade. How are you?
Jade Hi, fine thanks.
Presenter And what do you think of adult education courses?
Jade Oh, I think they're a great way to learn new skills. I wanted to make my own jewellery so I joined a course at Hartstown Community School – this is my second year. I go on Tuesday evening for two hours. It isn't expensive and I really enjoy it because the people are really friendly. My friends love my course, too, because now I make jewellery for them!
Presenter Thank you Jade. Now to caller two, Marco. Why did you decide to do a course, Marco?
Marco Er. Well I'm from Italy, but I work in Kildare now and I don't know many people. I want to make new friends. My class is Zumba – it's an exercise class. The first class was last Wednesday. It was great fun – there were about 16 students – and our teacher was very good. We all had coffee together after the class.
Presenter That sounds great, Marco. I hope you make lots of new friends. We have Dermot from Cork. Hi Dermot. Tell us about your course.
Dermot Hi. Well, I'm doing a course to get a qualification. My company has an office in Mexico and I want to work there so I go to a Spanish course on Mondays and Thursdays.
Presenter Do you think the courses are a good idea, Dermot?
Dermot Oh, I think they're great. There's a lot of homework on a course like mine – and I have an exam at the end of the year, but I really enjoy going to the college.
Presenter Good luck with your exam Dermot and thank you for talking to me. For information about adult education courses in your area, visit the Learning Ireland website. Now for a song...

Page 16, Exercises 3c & 4

2.7

Presenter Our next topic is adult learning. It's autumn now and many adult education classes are starting. Did you know that there are over 5,700 classes at schools and colleges here in Ireland? There are lots of different courses to choose from – you can learn to write a book, play the guitar, or speak a foreign language. Today, we want you to tell other listeners about your courses.

Unit 3 Work

Page 18, Exercise 2a

3.1

1   mechanic
2   cleaner
3   pilot
4   photographer
5   student
6   journalist
7   chef
8   businesswoman
9   musician
10 dentist
11 nurse
12 hairdresser

Page 18, Exercise 2b

3.2

cleaner
pilot
student
journalist
chef
businesswoman
dentist
nurse
photographer
mechanic
musician

Page 19, Exercises 7a & b

3.3

1 A Do you get up early in the morning?
   B No, I don't.
2 A Does this phone have a camera?
   B No, it doesn't.
3 A Does his daughter play a musical instrument?
   B Yes, she does.
4 A Do your neighbours have a dog?
   B No, they don't.
5 A Do you and John read newspapers?
   B Yes, we do.
6 A Does her brother like being alone?
   B Yes, he does.

Page 21, Exercise 4b

3.4

1 A What do you do?
   B I'm a police officer.
2 A Where do you work?
   B I work in St Leonards Police Station in Edinburgh.
3 A Why do you like your job?

89

- B It's interesting. My days are never the same.
4 A Who do you work with?
- B I work with lots of different people – police officers, people in the city, school children.
5 A When do you start work?
- B Well sometimes I start at 7 a.m. and work until 5 p.m. or sometimes I work nights - that means I work from 10 p.m. until 7 a.m.
6 A How often do you have meetings?
- B Oh, we have meetings every day, when we arrive at the station.
7 A What do you do after work?
- B Well, I walk a lot. I often go to Portobello Beach with my son- it's really nice there in winter and in summer.
8 A What time do you usually go to bed?
- B I'm usually tired after work, so I always go to bed early.

Page 21, Exercises 5b, 6a & b
3.5))
1 Where does he work?
2 When do they finish work?
3 Who do you work with?
4 How often does she use English at work?
5 What time does the shop close?
6 What do they usually have for lunch?
7 Where do I go for the meeting?
8 Why does he want to learn Chinese?
9 When do we have lunch?
10 Who lives in this house?

Page 23, Exercise 1b
3.6))
1 Could we have two tickets to see *Batman*, please?
2 Could you spell 'author', please?
3 Can I join the library, please?
4 Can I use your pencil, please?
5 Could you tell us where the station is, please?
6 Could I pay for my meal with my credit card, please?

Page 23, Exercise 2b
3.9))
1 Yes, of course.
2 I'm afraid not.
3 No, I'm sorry but...
4 Sure.
5 Yes, that's fine.

Unit 4 Places and things

Page 24, Exercise 3a
4.1))
a theatre
b campsite
c hotel
d airport
e restaurant
f museum
g hospital
h hairdresser's
i chemist

Page 24, Exercise 3b
4.2))
theatre
campsite
airport
restaurant
hospital
hairdresser's
chemist
hotel
museum

Page 25, Exercise 6b
4.3))
1 A Excuse me. Is there a tourist information centre in the town?
- B Yes, there is. It's just near the railway station.
2 A Is there a cinema in the town centre?
- B No, I'm sorry, there isn't. But there's a theatre.
3 A Are there any nice restaurants near here?
- B Yes, there are. There's the Lanterna Restaurant in Queen Street and Nico's in Westgate.
4 A Is there a campsite near the beach?
- B Yes, there is. The Sunny Days Campsite is near the beach.
5 A Are there any bookshops in the village?
- B No, I'm afraid there aren't.
6 A Are there many things to see in the town?
- B Yes, there are. There are lots of things to see and do here.

Page 26, Exercise 1b
4.4))
1 a house
2 a garage
3 a flat
4 a bedroom
5 a kitchen
6 a toilet
7 a living room
8 a bathroom
9 an office
10 a dining room

Page 27, Exercises 8a, b & c
4.5))
1 My house is next to the park.
2 There's a supermarket opposite the cinema.
3 Do you have a map of the city?
4 Is there an airport near your town?
5 The students are in a classroom on the second floor.

Page 29, Exercise 1b
4.6))
1 on the left
2 at the end of the road
3 take the first left
4 on the corner
5 turn right
6 go straight on
7 take the second left
8 go past the cinema

Page 29, Exercise 2b
4.7))
1 A Excuse me, how do we get to the Opal Centre.
- B Go out of the main door and turn right. Go straight on, past the theatre. It's on the left.
2 A Excuse me, could you give us some directions, please?
- B Yes, of course. How can I help you?
- A Thanks. We want to get to the hospital.
- B OK, well go out of the tourist information centre and turn right. Take the second road on the right. Turn left at the end of the road into Harlequin Street. Go straight ahead for ten minutes. Take the third turning on the right. It's on Opal Street on the left.
3 A Excuse me, where's the school?

90

B Go out of the main door and turn right. Take the first road on the left, then turn right into Kaolin Street. Go straight on for ten minutes. It's on the corner of Kaolin Street and Opal Street.

Unit 5 Clothes and shopping

Page 33, Exercises 6a & b

5.1
1 **A** Can we book the theatre tickets online?
  B No, but we can book them by phone.
2 **A** Can he play a musical instrument?
  B Yes, he can.
3 **A** I can't pay with my credit card.
  B That's OK, you can pay with cash.
  A No, I can't. I haven't got any cash.

Page 34, Exercise 1b

5.2
1 hat
2 tie
3 suit
4 trousers
5 umbrella
6 hoodie
7 scarf
8 jacket
9 gloves
10 jeans
11 trainers
12 glasses
13 coat
14 dress
15 jewellery
16 shoes
17 top
18 skirt
19 T-shirt
20 shorts
21 socks

Page 37, Exercise 2b

5.3
Customer Do you sell batteries?
Assistant Yes, we do. What kind do you want?
Customer Er … AAA, please – they're for my camera.
Assistant That's £4.50, please.
Customer Can I have two packets?
Assistant That's nine pounds. Would you like a bag?
Customer Yes, please. Just a small one.
Assistant And would you like your receipt in the bag?
Customer Yes, please.

Unit 6 The past

Page 39, Exercises 4b & c

6.1
1 I was tired last night.
2 Was I tired last night?
3 Yes, I was.
4 No, I wasn't.
5 They were at home last night.
6 Were they at home last night?
7 Yes, they were.
8 No, they weren't.

Page 39, Exercises 5a & b

6.2
1 **A** Was Elvis Presley famous?
  B Yes, he was.
2 **A** Why was the doctor at your house?
  B My husband was sick.
3 **A** Where were you yesterday?
  B We were at work.
4 **A** Were the teachers at your first school nice?
  B Yes, they were.
5 **A** When were you born?
  B I was born in 1992.

Page 40, Exercises 4b & c

6.3
1 /d/ changed returned started
2 /t/ called looked thanked
3 /ɪd/ collected finished included
4 /t/ worked liked posted
5 /d/ believed noticed prepared
6 /ɪd/ wanted needed used
7 /d/ waited received moved
8 /ɪd/ responded watched shouted
9 /t/ noticed practised turned

Page 42, Exercises 3a & b

6.4
1 He's a bit unfriendly.
2 Those bags are quite cheap.
3 She's really friendly.
4 This is a very interesting article.

Page 43, Exercise 2b

6.5
1 That's awful!
2 What a nightmare!
3 Really?
4 That's great!
5 That's terrible!
6 That's amazing!
7 Poor you!
8 That's brilliant!
9 Oh no!

Page 43, Exercise 3b

6.6
1 **A** My interview went really well. They offered me the job.
  B That's brilliant!
2 **A** Julia and Mark are getting married.
  B That's great!
3 **A** Our new neighbours moved into the house next door yesterday.
  B Really?
4 **A** I've got a cold.
  B Poor you!
5 **A** The bus is late again.
  B Oh no!
6 **A** Our holiday was terrible! The hotel was awful, the people were really unfriendly, and it rained every day so we couldn't go to the beach.
  B What a nightmare!
7 **A** My grandfather is 102 years old today.
  B That's amazing!
8 **A** Ken is really unhappy. The company he worked for closed last week and now he's unemployed.
  B That's awful!

Page 44, Exercise 3

6.7
Thank you for choosing the Stratford-upon-Avon audio walking tour. The walking tour takes two hours, but you can stop and visit some of the buildings and places of interest on the way.

We start our tour at the tourist information centre on Bridgefoot. Go out of the door and turn right. Go straight on for ten minutes. When you get to Henley Street go past the post office and the library. The next building on your right is William Shakespeare's Birthplace. Shakespeare was born there. The house is open to visitors from March to November.

Opposite Shakespeare's Birthplace is a small street called The Minories. Walk down here and turn left into Wood Street. At the end of Wood Street, turn right and walk to Nash House. Nash's House was the home of Shakespeare's granddaughter, Elizabeth. It was next to New Place – the house where Shakespeare died. Nash's House and New Place are open from March to November, too.

After Nash's House go straight on and the next building in Church Street is the old grammar school where Shakespeare was a student. It is still a school today.

Now, walk to the end of Church Street and go left. Walk past Hall's Croft – which was once the home of Shakespeare's daughter, Susanna. At Avonbank Gardens turn left and soon you can see the river. Walk along the river for 10 minutes. The next big building you see is the Royal Shakespeare Theatre. You can visit the theatre or have a meal in the theatre restaurant. In the evening you can see a play by Shakespeare. The theatre is usually very busy, so it's a good idea to buy tickets early.

In front of the theatre is Bancroft Gardens. Why not sit in the gardens and relax after your walk?

We hope you enjoyed your walking tour of Stratford-upon-Avon. Please write and tell us.

Unit 7 Health and fitness

Page 47, Exercises 6a & b

7.1))

1	taught	bought	rode
2	chose	put	wrote
3	said	felt	heard
4	came	drank	sang
5	took	flew	put
6	made	ate	caught

Page 48, Exercise 1b

7.2))

jog, cycle, run, ski, swim
go fishing, go to the gym
play basketball, play football, play tennis
do judo, do yoga

Page 51, Exercise 1b

7.3))

1 A What's your opinion of video exercise games?
   B They're OK. I've got a dance video that I use sometimes.
   A My kids want one of those tennis games – they say the games are a good way to keep fit, but I don't know about that. They can play tennis in the park.
   B Yes, but only in the summer! With a video game you can exercise inside all year.
   A That's true, but I think children today spend a lot of time in front of computer and TV screens and they need to do more things outside. Things were different when we were kids.
   B I agree with you. But the world is a different place now.
2 A What do you think of this company in London? They use mobile phone technology to check what their workers eat, when they exercise, and how they sleep. And they also give them an exercise plan. I think it's a great idea.
   B I don't agree with you.
   A Why not?
   B Well, for me, people's health is their business.
   A I don't know about that. When people aren't healthy they can't work and companies lose money.
   B That's right, of course. But do people really want their bosses to tell them what to eat and when to exercise?
   A Maybe not.

Unit 8 Travel and transport

Page 53, Exercise 5b

8.1))

Jeff Hi, Anna. When did you get back from your holiday?
Anna Last night. I'm really tired though – it was a long flight back.
Jeff Oh dear. Did you have a good time in the USA?
Anna Yes, I did, thanks. I had a fantastic time.
Jeff Did John go with you?
Anna No, he didn't, unfortunately. He had to work, so I went with Jenny – she's an old friend from university.
Jeff Oh right. So, what did you do?
Anna Well, first we flew to Boston, then we rented a car and drove down the coast to Miami.
Jeff Really? How far did you drive?
Anna It was about 1300 miles, I think.
Jeff Wow! And did you stay in hotels?
Anna Sometimes, but usually we went to campsites or small guest houses. It was good because we met lots of people that way.
Jeff So what was your favourite place?
Anna It's a bit difficult to say because we had a great time everywhere, but my favourite place was probably South Carolina - it was really beautiful and I loved Charleston.

Page 53, Exercises 6a & b

8.2))

1 Where in Morocco did they stay?
2 Did he take lots of photos in Marrakech?
3 What did you think of the local food?
4 Did I leave the camera in the hotel?
5 How many nights did we spend in Fez?
6 How did she travel from Rabat to Casablanca?

Page 55, Exercises 6a & b

8.3))

1 You should buy a travel card.
2 You have to buy a ticket.
3 You should wear your seat belt.
4 You shouldn't put your bag there.
5 You have to show your passport.
6 You shouldn't drive when you're tired.
7 You don't have to pay to visit the museum.
8 You don't have to come with me.
9 You should take a map with you.

Page 57, Exercise 2b

8.4))

Ticket seller Good morning. How can I help you?
Adam Hello. I want to get to Cape Town.
Ticket seller OK. When would you like to travel?
Adam Tomorrow if possible. When's the next train?
Ticket seller The next one leaves the day after tomorrow, on Tuesday at 13.09.
Adam OK, and how long does it take?
Ticket seller About 26 hours. It arrives at 15.30 on Wednesday.
Adam Right. How much is a sleeper ticket?
Ticket seller Would you like a single or a return?
Adam Just a single please.
Ticket seller OK, then tourist class tickets cost 600 rand. There aren't any first class sleepers on the train.
Adam 600 rand ... OK. Which platform does the train leave from?
Ticket seller It goes from that platform over there.
Adam Thank you.

AUDIOSCRIPTS

Unit 9 Cooking and eating

Page 61, Exercise 7a
9.1
1. There isn't any rice in the cupboard.
   Can I have some rice from the cupboard?
   There's some rice in the cupboard.
   Is there any rice in the cupboard?
2. There's some milk in the fridge.
   Is there any milk in the fridge?
   Can I have some milk from the fridge?
   There isn't any milk in the fridge.

Page 64, Exercise 1b
9.2
1. five million
2. three quarters
3. the fourteenth of July
4. nineteen sixty-seven
5. three point nine
6. eighteen per cent
7. seventy three degrees Celsius

Page 64, Exercise 2b
9.3
a. fifth
b. half
c. seven thousand, four hundred and ninety-one kilometres
d. two hundred million
e. eighty-seven per cent
f. two million, seven hundred thousand
g. eighteen twenty-two
h. the sixth of September
i. twenty-twelve
j. five point seven million
k. thirty metres
l. thirty degrees Celsius

Page 65, Exercise 1
9.4
Jack This is my favourite restaurant. I hope you like it.
Anna Oh, I love Italian food.
Waiter Would you like to order lunch now?
Jack Yes, please.
Waiter Would you like a starter?
Jack Yes, please. Could I have the soup of the day, please?
Waiter And for you madam?
Anna Uh … Could I have a mixed salad, please?
Waiter And what would you like for your main course?
Anna Uh … Could I have the pasta with mushroom sauce?
Waiter Of course, and for you sir?
Jack Um … The grilled fish for me.
Waiter Would you like any side dishes with that?
Jack Can I have some rice and some steamed vegetables?
Waiter Certainly. And would you like something to drink?
Jack Can we have a bottle of water, please?

Page 65, Exercises 2a & b
9.5
1. Would you like to order lunch now?
2. Would you like a starter?
3. Could I have the soup of the day, please?
4. Could I have a mixed salad, please?
5. Could I have the pasta with mushroom sauce?
6. Would you like any side dishes with that?
7. Can I have some rice and some steamed vegetables?
8. And would you like something to drink?
9. Can we have a bottle of water, please?

Unit 10 The world around us

Page 67, Exercises 7a & b
10.1
1. This hotel is more expensive than that hotel.
2. China is bigger than Thailand.
3. Winter is colder than summer.
4. I think surfing is better than skiing.
5. Travelling by train is more interesting than flying.
6. Some people are friendlier than others.

Page 69, Exercises 7a & b
10.2
1. the fastest
2. the oldest
3. the most dangerous
4. the dirtiest
5. the hottest
6. the best

Page 71, Exercise 3b
10.3
1. I think we should take a torch because it's dark at night.
2. I prefer to take a first aid kit instead of a stove because we can use wood to make a fire.
3. The most useful things to take are the sleeping bags because it's cold at night.
4. A map is more important than a lighter because it's easy to get lost.
5. Using a stove is a better idea than making a fire because it's difficult to make a fire in the rain.

Page 72, Exercises 3 & 4b
10.4
Steve Good morning and welcome to Steve in the Kitchen. My name's Steve Shaw. In today's show we have two of the country's top chefs. Let me introduce my first guest, Marcus Candy, from Le Resto, one of the country's top restaurants. Hello, Marcus and welcome to the studio. How are you?
Marcus Fine, thanks Steve. It's really good to be here.
Steve What are you cooking for us today?
Marcus Well, everyone loves roast chicken and today I'm doing my own special milk chicken with lemon roasted potatoes.
Steve That sounds very nice. Is the recipe difficult?
Marcus No, it isn't – it's very simple. Anyone can follow it and make a perfect milk chicken.
Steve Does it take a long time to prepare?
Marcus No, not long. You need 10 minutes to get everything ready, then 45 minutes to roast the chicken in the oven. And while the chicken is roasting, you can make the roasted lemon potatoes.
Steve OK, while Marcus is cooking we're going to be reading and answering your food questions, so please email or text them to our website. OK, Marcus let's get cooking. What ingredients are you using?
Marcus Well for the milk chicken, you need a chicken, half a litre of milk, a spoon of olive oil, ten pieces of garlic, salt, and some herbs.
Steve Do you want me to help?
Marcus Yes, please. I need you to wash the chicken first. Then use this knife to cut it into two halves.
Steve Here you are.
Marcus Thanks. Now I'm putting some olive oil over the chicken and some salt – sea salt is the best salt to use. The

93

next thing we do is put the grill on and grill the chicken for five minutes until it is nice and brown.

Steve Is this one of your own recipes, Marcus?

Marcus No, this is one of my mother's. She made it on Sundays, when all the family were together. It was one of my favourites and I thought your viewers would like it. OK, the chicken looks ready now, so I'm going to put it in this roasting pan and add the garlic and herbs. Then we put the milk over the chicken, and put the whole thing in the oven for about 45 minutes.

Marcus Now for the lemon roasted potatoes – this is a Greek recipe, also one of my mother's. For this you need …

Page 72, Exercise 5a

10.5))
1 How are you?
2 What are you cooking for us today?
3 Is the recipe difficult?
4 Does it take a long time to prepare?
5 What ingredients are you using?
6 Do you want me to help?
7 Is this one of your own recipes, Marcus?

Unit 11 Working together

Page 75, Exercises 7a & b

11.1))
1 What are you going to do?
2 I'm going to visit my grandparents tomorrow.
3 Is Annie going to drive to Berlin?
4 We aren't going to have a holiday this year.
5 Liam is going to cook dinner for us.
6 Ella isn't going to come to the theatre with us.

Page 75, Exercises 8a & b

11.2))
1 I'm not going to go out.
2 He isn't going to call you.
3 We aren't going to buy it.
4 They aren't going to come.
5 You aren't going to have much time.
6 She isn't going to make dinner.

Page 76, Exercise 1b

11.3))
1 website
2 smartphone
3 app
4 gps
5 text
6 tablet

Page 76, Exercises 3b & c

11.4))
1 www.nelsonmandela.org (w w w dot nelson mandela dot org)
2 anton@russorest.com (anton at Russorest dot com)
3 www.bbc.co.uk/news (w w w dot bbc dot co dot uk forward slash news)
4 joel_kubi@mailbox.com joel underscore kubi at mailbox dot com)
5 www.whitehouse.gov/ (w w w dot Whitehouse dot gov forward slash)
6 mark-derby@mailbox.au (Mark dash Derby at mailbox dot A U)

Page 79, Exercise 3b

11.5))
A This is the list of the things for the youth-club trip to the coast.
B OK, this looks fine, but we'll need some sports equipment, too, so we can play football and volleyball on the beach. Shall I write that down?
A Good idea. Use my pen. Right, let's go through the list. First, we'll need to organize a bus to take everyone there.
C Why don't I do that? I've got more time than you and I can phone the bus company this afternoon.
A Perfect. Now what about a poster to tell everyone about the trip? I can write the text but I'm not very good at art.
C Let me help you. We can design the poster together on my new tablet.
A Thanks, Carlos.
B Would you like me to print the posters? I can use the printer at the university.
A OK - I'll email the design to you when it's ready. Now, what's next?
C It looks like it's going to be a long evening. Shall I make a drink?
B Oh, I'd love a coffee.

Unit 12 Culture and the arts

Page 81, Exercises 4 & 5

12.1))
1 We haven't seen Jane
2 She's won a prize.
3 He hasn't been to university.
4 They haven't finished work.
5 You've fixed my computer.
6 I've joined a gym.

Page 81, Exercise 8b

12.2))
1 A Have you seen the new *Star Wars* film?
  B Yes, I went to the cinema with Alex to see it.
2 A Do you want to go to the theatre next week? The new Andrew Lloyd Webber musical is on.
  B That sounds great. I saw his last musical and I loved it.
3 A I'd love to learn to play the guitar like you.
  B Really? I can teach you if you want.
4 A Where's Ping? I haven't seen her today.
  B She's gone to a rock concert in Berlin.
5 A That's a lovely picture. How did you learn to draw like that?
  B Thanks, I had some drawing lessons last summer.
6 A I really want to go to the Glastonbury festival this year, but I can't get a ticket.
  B I bought my ticket last month - I love going to music festivals. My cousin's playing in a band there this year.

Page 85, Exercise 1b

12.3))
1 Hi Artem, it's Megan. Is Ellie there?
2 Could you ask him to call me back, please?
3 She's not here at the moment.
4 Hang on a minute. I'll just get her.
5 Can you tell her to call me back, please?
6 I'm afraid he's out of the office.
7 Could I have your number, please?
8 Hello. Could I speak to the manager, please?
9 I'm afraid he's unable to take your call at the moment.
10 Hold on.

94

AUDIOSCRIPTS

Page 85, Exercise 3b

12.4

1   **A** Hello
    B Hi Alison, it's Bashir. Is Chris there?
    A Sorry, he's not here at the moment.
    B OK. Can you tell him to call me back please?
    A Sure, oh hold on, he's just come back. Chris, Bashir wants to speak to you.
    C Hi, Bashir.
    B Hi, Chris. Have you booked the restaurant for Alison's surprise birthday party?
    C No, I haven't had time. I'll do it now and I'll call you back in a minute.

2   **A** Good afternoon. How can I help you?
    B Hello. Could I speak to the restaurant manager, please?
    A I'm afraid she's unable to take your call at the moment. Can I help?
    B Maybe. I'd like to book a table for twelve for tomorrow night.
    A Oh, you'll need to speak to the restaurant manager about that.
    B Could you ask her to call me back, please?
    A Yes of course. Could I have your name and telephone number, please?
    B Yes, it's Chris Brown and the number is 072 …

Answer key

Unit 1 Your world

1.1 Multicultural cities page 4

Vocabulary countries, nationalities and languages

1a 1 the USA – American
    2 Mexico – Mexican
    3 Britain – British
    4 France – French
    5 Italy – Italian
    6 Poland – Polish
    7 Greece – Greek
    8 Turkey – Turkish
    9 UAE – Emirati
   10 Pakistan – Pakistani
   11 China – Chinese
   12 Vietnam – Vietnamese

2   1 the USA – English
    2 Mexico – Spanish
    3 Britain – English
    4 France – French
    5 Italy – Italian
    6 Poland – Polish
    7 Greece – Greek
    8 Turkey – Turkish
    9 UAE – Arabic
   10 Pakistan – Urdu
   11 Vietnam – Vietnamese
   12 China – Chinese

3a

O	Oo	oO
French Greek	English Spanish Polish Turkish Urdu	Chinese

Ooo	oOoo	oooO
Arabic	Italian	Vietnamese

4   1 China
    2 Chinese
    3 Chinese/English
    4 English/Chinese
    5 Senegal
    6 French
    7 Senegalese
    8 country
    9 city
   10 nationality
   11 language

Grammar present simple *to be*

5   1 aren't   5 isn't
    2 'm   6 is
    3 isn't   7 're
    4 are   8 aren't

6   1 Are you from Thailand?
       Yes, I am.
    2 Is Mary a student? No, she isn't.
    3 Are Lily and Sergei married?
       Yes, they are.
    4 Is your house near a supermarket?
       Yes, it is.
    5 Are the children at school?
       No, they aren't.
    6 Are you and Tony Irish?
       No, we aren't.
    7 Is Naila's husband from Iraq?
       Yes, he is.
    8 Are we late? Yes, you are.
    9 Are you our new teacher?
       No, I'm not.

7a 1 What's your name?
    2 Are you French?
    3 What's your nationality?
    4 Where is your home?
    5 Are your neighbours French-Canadian?
    6 Are you married?
    7 Are you a teacher?

8   1 is Pakistani
    2 are Spanish
    3 are Japanese
    4 is German
    5 is Italian
    6 are South Korean

1.2 Family page 6

Grammar possessive determiners

1a 1 e   5 b
    2 a   6 d
    3 g   7 c
    4 f

2   1 My, I   5 Its, It's
    2 Our   6 She, Her
    3 They   7 his
    4 you, your

3   1 your   5 Their
    2 my   6 its
    3 his   7 her
    4 our

Vocabulary family

4   1 husband, daughter, son-in-law, grandfather, cousin, wife
    2 wife, brother, brother-in-law

5a

Male	Female	Male or female
husband son-in-law grandfather brother brother-in-law	daughter wife	cousin

5b

Male	Female	Male or female
father grandfather grandson half-brother nephew son step-father uncle	aunt granddaughter grandmother mother niece	child grandparent parent

6   1 aunt and nephew
    2 wife and husband
    3 granddaughter and grandfather
    4 uncle and nephew
    5 father and daughter / parent and child
    6 brothers
    7 sister-in-law and brother-in-law

Grammar possessive 's

7   Sentences with a possessive 's:
    1, 3, 6, 8

8   1 Sancho's   5 grandfather's
    2 Maria's   6 mother's/mum's
    3 Isabel's   7 Sancho's
    4 son's

9a 1 are, our
    2 They're, Their
    3 He's, His
    4 You're, your
    5 's, 's

10a 4 He's/His

96

ANSWER KEY

1.3 Vocabulary development page 8

Vocabulary regular and irregular plurals

1.
   1. *dictionaries*
   2. bookshelves
   3. boxes of chocolates
   4. brushes
   5. football pitches
   6. buses

2.
   1. *cities*
   2. presidents
   3. neighbours
   4. classes
   5. children, adults
   6. babies
   7. men, women
   8. people
   9. cars, roads

Vocabulary review

3.

Country	Nationality	Language
Britain	*British*	*English*
China	Chinese	Chinese
France	French	French
Germany	German	German
Italy	Italian	Italian
Mexico	Mexican	Spanish
Pakistan	Pakistani	Urdu
Poland	Polish	Polish
Turkey	Turkish	Turkish
the UAE	Emirati	Arabic
the USA	American	English
Vietnam	Vietnamese	Vietnamese

4.
   1. *father*
   2. wife
   3. grandfather
   4. granddaughter
   5. son
   6. sister
   7. uncle
   8. niece
   9. sister-in-law
   10. half-brother
   11. step-brother

1.4 Speaking and writing page 9

Speaking asking for personal information and checking you understand

1.
   1. *an Arabic*
   2. Jackie
   3. surname
   4. Australian
   5. teacher
   6. jackie1@alamilla.co.uk
   7. email address

2a.
   1. *What's your name?*
   2. How do you spell your surname?
   3. What's your nationality?
   4. What's your job?
   5. What's your email address?
   6. Sorry, can you repeat your first name, please?

3.
   a 1   d 2
   b 4   e 6
   c 5   f 3

Writing a personal profile

4a. My <u>n</u>ame is <u>M</u>aria <u>M</u>artinez. <u>M</u>y parents are Mexican but <u>I</u> am <u>A</u>merican. I'm fluent in <u>S</u>panish and English. I live in Los <u>A</u>ngeles.

4b.
   1 *s*   4 F
   2 U   5 w
   3 O   6 I

Unit 2 My day

2.1 A day in the life of a scientist page 10

Grammar present simple and adverbs of frequency

1.
   1. *speak*   8. writes
   2. study   9. visits
   3. are   10. meet
   4. live   11. think
   5. starts   12. love
   6. gets up   13. go
   7. makes   14. have

2.
   1. *loves*   5. works
   2. drives   6. relaxes
   3. studies   7. writes
   4. teaches

3b.

/s/	/z/	/ɪz/
works	*loves*	teaches
writes	drives	relaxes
	studies	

4.
   1. *Dr Abacha always gets up early in the morning.*
   2. She usually drives to the hospital.
   3. She sometimes works at the weekend.
   4. She often has meetings with other doctors.
   5. She hardly ever finishes work before 7 p.m.
   6. She never goes to the beach.
   7. She is always tired in the evening.

5.
   1. *You're never late for work.*
   2. Manuel often cooks dinner for his family.
   3. Nurses never relax at work.
   4. It's always very hot in summer in Dubai.
   5. I usually listen to music in the car.
   6. Ivan hardly ever writes emails to his friends.
   7. We sometimes see seals on the beach near our house.

Vocabulary daily activities

6.
   a *make*   g arrive
   b have   h get
   c go   i listen to
   d have   j see
   e watch   k go
   f read   l play

7.
   1. *get up*
   2. have a shower
   3. makes breakfast
   4. go to work
   5. listen to music
   6. have lunch
   7. arrive home
   8. see friends
   9. play video games
   10. reads a book
   11. watch TV
   12. go to bed

2.2 Spending time page 12

Vocabulary telling the time

1a.
   1. *half past nine*
   2. twenty-five to five
   3. ten past six
   4. quarter to eleven
   5. twenty-five past four
   6. twenty past seven
   7. five to ten
   8. ten to two
   9. quarter past one
   10. twenty to three
   11. five past eight
   12. twelve o'clock

2.
   1. *twenty to five*
   2. twenty past seven
   3. half past eleven
   4. quarter to seven
   5. quarter past ten
   6. twenty-five past eight
   7. five to four
   8. ten past two

3a.
   1. *ten to*
   2. twenty-five past
   3. quarter to nine
   4. twenty past
   5. quarter past

97

6 half past
7 half past seven
8 twelve o'clock

Grammar present simple negative

4 1 *don't*   5 don't
   2 doesn't   6 don't
   3 don't   7 doesn't
   4 don't   8 doesn't

5a 1 *We don't work in a factory.*
   2 You don't know his sister.
   3 He doesn't speak Thai.
   4 I don't have a dog.
   5 They don't study languages.
   6 It doesn't go to Leeds.
   7 She doesn't get up at 6 a.m.
   8 We don't stay at home.

6 1 *It doesn't spend a lot of time in the USA.*
   2 It has six labs.
   3 They don't cook their own meals.
   4 They don't have a lot of free time.
   5 They use the labs on the boat.
   6 She meets scientists from other countries.
   7 She sometimes feels seasick.
   8 She doesn't study sea animals.

2.3 Vocabulary development page 14

Vocabulary verb + preposition phrases

1 1 *f*   6 h
   2 d   7 e
   3 j   8 g
   4 c   9 b
   5 i   10 a

2 1 *with*   6 at
   2 at   7 for
   3 for   8 to
   4 at   9 about
   5 to   10 for

3 1 *think about*
   2 arrive at
   3 wait for
   4 talk to
   5 listen to
   6 look at
   7 ask for
   8 pay for

Vocabulary review

4 1 *get up*
   2 make breakfast
   3 go to work/college
   4 have lunch/dinner
   5 see friends
   6 go home

7 go to bed
8 watch TV/a film
9 play video games
10 have a shower
11 listen to music
12 read a book

5 1 *one o'clock*
   2 five past one
   3 ten past one
   4 quarter past one
   5 twenty past one
   6 twenty-five past one
   7 half past one
   8 twenty-five to two
   9 twenty to two
   10 quarter to two
   11 ten to two
   12 five to two
   13 two o'clock

2.4 Speaking and writing page 15

Speaking making suggestions and arrangements

1a 1 *Would you like to go out for dinner tonight?*
   2 I'm sorry, but I'm busy this evening.
   3 Are you free tomorrow?
   4 Yes, I'd love to.
   5 Let's meet at the train station.
   6 Do you want to try that new restaurant near the park?
   7 Where shall we meet?
   8 Yes, that sounds nice.
   9 What time do you want to eat?
   10 Thanks, but I'm afraid I have plans tonight.

2a

Making suggestions/ arrangements	Accepting	Refusing
Would you like to go out for dinner tonight? Are you free tomorrow? Let's meet at the train station. Do you want to try that new restaurant near the park? Where shall we meet? What time do you want to eat?	Yes, I'd love to. Yes, that sounds nice.	I'm sorry, but I'm busy this evening. Thanks, but I'm afraid I have plans tonight.

3a 1 *Would you like to go out for dinner tonight?*
   2 Are you free tomorrow?
   3 Do you want to try that new restaurant near the park?

4 What time do you want to eat?
5 Where shall we meet?
6 Let's meet at the train station.

Writing describe where you live

4 1 *because*   3 and
   2 but   4 or

5 1 but   3 and
   2 because   4 or

2.5 Listening for pleasure page 16

1 1 get a qualification
   2 learn a new skill
   3 make new friends

2 1 a jewellery-making class
   2 an exercise class
   3 a language class

3b 1 *autumn*   5 guitar
   2 know   6 foreign
   3 schools   7 listeners
   4 write

4 1 *autum(n)*   5 g(u)itar
   2 (k)now   6 foreig(n)
   3 school(s)   7 listen(e)rs
   4 wr(i)te

Review: Units 1 and 2 page 17

Grammar

1 1 *Angela isn't from Greece – she's Italian.*
   2 What's your daughter's name?
   3 My first language is Turkish.
   4 I'm always in my office on Monday morning.
   5 We never drive to work because we don't have a car.
   6 Sanjay and his parents are from India.
   7 Are you a student?
   8 Dan and Emma are Jane and Simon's children.

2 1 *works*   6 don't live
   2 doesn't like 7 teaches
   3 closes   8 studies
   4 go   9 phone
   5 have   10 travel

Vocabulary

3 1 *American*   5 wife
   2 nationality   6 Urdu
   3 son   7 children
   4 cities   8 the UAE

98

ANSWER KEY

4
1 *b* 5 f
2 h 6 c
3 e 7 g
4 a 8 d

Speaking

5
1 *Would* 5 let's
2 sorry 6 address
3 want 7 repeat
4 love 8 See

Unit 3 The world of work

3.1 Jobs page 18

Vocabulary jobs

1
1 *mechanic*
2 cleaner
3 pilot
4 photographer
5 student
6 journalist
7 chef
8 businesswoman
9 musician
10 dentist
11 nurse
12 hairdresser

2a

Stress on first syllable	Stress on second syllable
cleaner	*mechanic*
pilot	photographer
student	musician
journalist	
chef	
dentist	
nurse	
hairdresser	

3a
1 *well-paid* 4 outside
2 inside 5 badly paid
3 hands 6 computer

3b
1 *businesswoman*
2 nurse
3 mechanic
4 photographer
5 cleaner
6 journalist

Grammar yes/no questions

4
1 *Are* 5 Do
2 Are 6 Do
3 Are 7 Do
4 Is 8 Does

5
1 *Do you walk a lot?*
2 Is Moscow very cold in winter?
3 Does the boss want to speak to me?
4 Am I late again?
5 Does it rain a lot in Ireland?
6 Do I need to finish this work today?

6
1 *No, I don't.*
2 No, it doesn't.
3 Yes, she does.
4 No, they don't.
5 Yes, we do.
6 Yes, he does.

7 In the short answers

8
1 *No, she doesn't.*
2 Yes, it is.
3 Yes, she does.
4 Yes, it does.
5 No, they aren't.
6 No, they don't.
7 Yes, they do.

3.2 What do you do? page 20

Vocabulary work

1
1 *places*
2 no job
3 people
4 hours
5 money
6 company/no company

2
1 *work for a company*
2 full-time
3 salary
4 colleagues
5 unemployed
6 hospital
7 manager
8 boss
9 office
10 earn
11 factory
12 long
13 retired
14 freelance
15 work for a magazine
16 home
17 part-time

Grammar Wh- questions

3
1 *f* 4 c
2 d 5 e
3 b 6 a

4a
1 *What* 5 When/What time
2 Where 6 How often
3 Why 7 What
4 Who 8 When/What time

5
1 *Where does he work?*
2 ✓
3 Who do you work with?
4 How often does she use English at work?
5 What time does the shop close?
6 What do they usually have for lunch?
7 ✓
8 Why does he want to learn Chinese?
9 When do you have dinner?
10 ✓

6a The intonation goes down.

7 In the short answers.

3.3 Vocabulary development page 22

Vocabulary -er suffix

1
1 *singer* 6 heater
2 computer 7 dancer
3 winner 8 cooker
4 painter 9 builder
5 baker

Vocabulary review

2
1 businessman
2 businesswoman
3 cleaner
4 dentist
5 hairdresser
6 journalist
7 mechanic
8 musician
9 nurse
10 pilot
11 photographer
12 chef
13 student

3
1 *computers*, hands
2 outside
3 inside
4 badly paid
5 well-paid

4
1 *unemployed*
2 a salary
3 colleagues
4 full-time, long hours
5 an office
6 home
7 a magazine

5
1 bake 10 make
2 begin 11 manage
3 build 12 paint
4 clean 13 play
5 cook 14 run
6 dance 15 sing
7 drive 16 teach
8 farm 17 win
9 heat 18 work

99

3.4 Speaking and writing page 23

Speaking making requests

1a 1 *Could we have two tickets to see Batman, please?*
2 Could you spell 'author', please?
3 Can I join the library, please?
4 Can I use your pencil, please?
5 Could you tell us where the station is, please?
6 Could I pay for my meal with my credit card, please?

2a 1 P   4 P
2 N   5 P
3 N

3a 1 *at work*   4 in a car park
2 in a shop   5 in a school
3 at home   6 in a café/restaurant

3b a *5*   d 2
b 3   e 4
c 1   f 6

Writing opening and closing an email

4 1 *Dear*   5 Hi
2 Can we   6 How are you
3 I'm free   7 Can I
4 Best wishes   8 Love

Unit 4 Places and things

4.1 Underground towns page 24

Vocabulary places in a town

1 1 *school*
2 a hospital
3 shops
4 a library
5 a cinema
6 swimming pool
7 a railway station
8 the roads
9 the tourist information centre
10 the museum

2 a *theatre*   f museum
b campsite   g hospital
c hotel   h hairdresser's
d airport   i chemist
e restaurant

3a

Stress on first syllable	Stress on second syllable
theatre	hotel
campsite	museum
airport	
restaurant	
hospital	
hairdresser's	
chemist	

Grammar there is/there are

4 1 *b*   4 e
2 f   5 c
3 a   6 d

5a 1 *There isn't a railway station.*
2 There's a museum.
3 There are three restaurants.
4 There's a supermarket.
5 There aren't any big hotels.
6 There isn't a hospital.
7 There are old buildings.
8 There aren't many people.
9 There's a tourist information centre.

6a 1 *Is there*, there is
2 Is there, there isn't
3 Are there, there are
4 Is there a, there is
5 any, there aren't
6 things, there are

4.2 Where I live page 26

Vocabulary rooms and furniture, prepositions of place

1a 1 *a house*   6 a toilet
2 a garage   7 a living room
3 a flat   8 a bathroom
4 a bedroom   9 an office
5 a kitchen   10 a dining room

2 1 *beds*   6 washing machine
2 cooker   7 shelf
3 fridge   8 sink
4 carpet   9 armchair
5 table

3a 1 *behind*   5 in front of
2 opposite   6 between
3 next to   7 under
4 above   8 on

4 1 *on*   6 on
2 under   7 In front of
3 behind   8 Next to
4 between   9 opposite
5 above

Grammar articles *a/an, the, –*

5 1 *Mumbai is an interesting city to visit.*
2 Is there an elevator in your building?
3 My parents have a house near the beach.
4 I have a big sofa in my living room.
5 You can visit an opal mine in Australia.
6 Is there a metro station near here?
7 There isn't an airport in my town.
8 There's a park in the town centre.

6 1 The Nile River is in ~~the~~ Africa.
2 There are lots of ~~the~~ flats in the building.
3 The capital of Thailand is ~~the~~ Bangkok.
4 The Prado Museum is in the centre of ~~the~~ Madrid.
5 We go to the cinema on ~~the~~ Saturdays.

7 1 *the*   9 the
2 a   10 the
3 the   11 –
4 a   12 –
5 an   13 a
6 a   14 the
7 –   15 a
8 –

8a 1 My house is next <u>to</u> <u>the</u> park.
2 There's a supermarket <u>opposite</u> <u>the</u> cinema.
3 <u>Do</u> <u>you</u> have <u>a</u> map <u>of</u> <u>the</u> city.
4 Is <u>there</u> <u>an</u> airport near your town?
5 <u>The</u> students <u>are</u> in <u>a</u> classroom on <u>the</u> second floor.

8b 1 *house, next, park*
2 supermarket, opposite, cinema
3 have, map, city
4 airport, near, town
5 students, classroom, second, floor

4.3 Vocabulary development page 28

Vocabulary opposite adjectives

1 1 *clean shoes*
2 a noisy child
3 a heavy box
4 a messy desk
5 a small dog
6 a new car

2 1 *dirty*   5 bad
2 beautiful   6 old-fashioned
3 long   7 difficult
4 fantastic

100

ANSWER KEY

Vocabulary review

4

Places to live	Places in the home	Furniture
flat house	bathroom bedroom dining room garage kitchen living room office toilet	*armchair* bed carpet cooker dishwasher fridge shelf sink table washing machine

5
1. *tidy*
2. dirty
3. short
4. cheap
5. noisy
6. easy
7. good
8. ugly
9. new
10. light
11. small
12. fantastic
13. modern

4.4 Speaking and writing page 29

Speaking asking for and giving directions

1a
1. *left*
2. end
3. first
4. corner
5. turn
6. straight
7. take
8. past

2a
1. the Opal Centre
2. the hospital
3. the school

Writing imperatives

3
1. Don't use
2. wash
3. Don't leave
4. clean
5. take
6. Don't forget

4.5 Reading for pleasure page 30

1
1. *an artist*
2. a painting
3. an exhibition
4. a theatre
5. a statue

3
1. *modern art*
2. statues
3. Museum of the City of New York
4. Museum of Modern Art (MOMA)
5. the USA

Review: Units 3 and 4 page 31

Grammar

1
1. e
2. a
3. h
4. d
5. b
6. f
7. c
8. g

2
1. *a*
2. the
3. an
4. the
5. a
6. a
7. there are
8. there aren't
9. there isn't
10. –
11. there's
12. –

Vocabulary

3
1. *businessman*
2. company
3. full-time
4. well-paid
5. colleagues
6. office
7. hospital
8. salary

4
1. *a factory*
2. a library
3. a kitchen
4. under
5. a shower

Speaking

5
1. *get to*, at the end of
2. Could I, That's fine
3. where's, go past, the right
4. Can you
5. near here, turn right

Unit 5 Clothes and shopping

5.1 Shopping page 32

Vocabulary shopping

1

Across	Down
1 *bread*	2 return
4 centre	3 meat
5 spend	5 sales
7 online	6 discount
8 cash	
9 magazine	

2
1. *cash*
2. butcher's
3. newsagent's
4. baker's
5. spend
6. shopping centres
7. online
8. discounts
9. sales
10. return

Grammar can/can't/could/couldn't

3
1. *couldn't pay, could pay*, can buy, can't use
2. can get, can go, could get, couldn't take
3. could get, couldn't shop, can't do, can find
4. could have, couldn't watch, can enjoy, can't remember
5. could eat, couldn't buy, can't go, can visit

4
1. *Could you get cash from machines in the 1880s? Yes, you could.*
2. Can he visit the museum on Sunday? Yes, he can.
3. Can I book the plane tickets online? Yes, I can.
4. Can we park in the centre of the town? No, we can't.
5. Could people shop online in the 1980s? No, they couldn't.
6. Could children play outside in the past? Yes, they could.

5
1. *Can you buy bread at the newsagent's?*
2. Could people spend euros in 1995?
3. Can you do this exercise? Yes, I can.
4. You couldn't use the internet in 1975.
5. You can't swim in the sea – it's dangerous.
6. People can buy most things online now.

6a
1. *U, U*
2. U, S
3. S, U, S

5.2 What is he wearing? page 34

Vocabulary clothes and accessories

1a
- coat *13*
- dress 14
- glasses 12
- gloves 9
- hat 1
- hoodie 6
- jacket 8
- jeans 10
- jewellery 15
- scarf 7
- shoes 16
- shorts 20
- skirt 18
- socks 21
- suit 3
- tie 2
- top 17
- trainers 11
- trousers 4
- T-shirt 19
- umbrella 5

2
1. *an umbrella*
2. jewellery
3. glasses
4. suit
5. gloves
6. neck
7. shoes
8. coat

Grammar present continuous

3
1. *'re buying*
2. 's working
3. 's wearing
4. 'm making
5. 're swimming
6. 're having
7. 're driving
8. 's raining

101

4
1 *Where are Allen and Daria going?*
2 Are you drinking my coffee?
3 He isn't listening to the teacher.
4 Is Ellie doing her homework?
5 I'm not enjoying this film.
6 It isn't snowing today, but it's cold.
7 Why are those people standing there?
8 We aren't working today.

Grammar present continuous or present simple

5
1 *drive, 'm taking*
2 works, 's relaxing
3 doesn't have, 's buying
4 're leaving, 's
5 're waiting, opens
6 are, going, want
7 's returning, doesn't like
8 's raining, carry

6
1 ✓
2 *is getting*
3 are helping
4 ✓
5 ✓
6 is wearing
7 is checking
8 ✓
9 ✓
10 ✓
11 are coming
12 are cooking

5.3 Vocabulary development page 36

Vocabulary adjectives and adverbs

1
1 *I can't run fast in these shoes.*
2 Sylvia can't see clearly without her glasses.
3 Peter and Jan work hard every day.
4 I always drive carefully.
5 Why do the trains always arrive late?
6 Please play quietly.
7 My sister cooks well.

2
1 *slow*
2 well
3 dangerously
4 correct
5 quiet
6 quickly
7 badly

Vocabulary review

3
1 *online*
2 cash
3 spend
4 shopping centre
5 the baker's
6 the newsagent's
7 return
8 the sales
9 the butcher's
10 a discount

4

Clothes	Accessories
coat	*glasses*
dress	gloves
hoodie	hat
jacket	jewellery
jeans	scarf
skirt	shoes
suit	socks
top	tie
trousers	trainers
T-shirt	umbrella

5
1 *badly*   7 well
2 careful   8 hard
3 clearly   9 late
4 dangerous 10 quickly
5 easy   11 quietly
6 fast   12 slow

5.4 Speaking and writing page 37

Speaking in a shop

1a
1 1 *Excuse*   5 off
  2 help   6 credit card
  3 How much 7 take
  4 discount

2 1 *Can*   5 close
  2 just   6 try
  3 need   7 changing rooms
  4 ask

2a
1 What kind do you want?
2 That's £4.50, please.
3 Would you like a bag?
4 And would you like your receipt in the bag?

Writing a product review

3
1 *I recommend it*
2 expensive
3 easy
4 great value
5 quickly

4
1 She's wearing a scarf, a hat and gloves today.
2 Shopping online is easy, cheap and you can return things that you don't like.
3 Jake's a good driver: he drives slowly, carefully and not too fast.

Unit 6 The past

6.1 Don't give up! page 38

Grammar was and were

1
1 *The co-founders of Microsoft were Bill Gates and Paul Allen.*
2 Was the restaurant expensive?
3 Harry's meal wasn't very good.
4 I was very tired last night.
5 Where were you yesterday?
6 We weren't late for work this morning.
7 Why was Vincent van Gogh famous?
8 I wasn't born in England.

2
1 *was*   6 wasn't
2 was   7 were
3 weren't   8 weren't
4 were   9 was
5 was   10 was

3
1 *Was; Yes, he was.*
2 Were; No, they weren't.
3 Were, Yes, they were.
4 Was; No, he wasn't.
5 Was; Yes, it was.

4a
1 *U*   5 U
2 U   6 U
3 S   7 S
4 S   8 S

5a
1 *U, S*   4 U, S
2 U, U   5 U, U
3 U, U

Vocabulary time expressions

6
1 *Jackie was in her office half an hour ago.*
2 The last London Olympics were in 2012.
3 There was an important football match last night.
4 We were in Spain last year.
5 I was very tired this morning.
6 Albert Einstein was born in the nineteenth century.
7 There was a staff meeting a few days ago.
8 She was in hospital two months ago.

7
1 *Jackie was in her office half an hour ago.*
2 I was very tired this morning.
3 There was an important football match last night.
4 There was a staff meeting a few days ago.

102

ANSWER KEY

5 She was in hospital two months ago.
6 We were in Spain last year.
7 The last London Olympics were in 2012.
8 Albert Einstein was born in the nineteenth century.

8 1 *in 2006*
2 last month
3 Two years ago
4 in the 19th century
5 a long time ago
6 Last year
7 in 1935
8 in the summer
9 last night

6.2 Stories page 40

Grammar past simple regular verbs

1 1 *carried*   7 looked
2 closed   8 loved
3 collected   9 played
4 copied   10 relaxed
5 earned   11 returned
6 enjoyed   12 tried

2 1 *wanted*   8 arrived
2 visited   9 noticed
3 waited   10 used
4 opened   11 decided
5 needed   12 talked
6 studied   13 liked
7 worked

3 1 *lived*   5 carried
2 believed   6 retired
3 listened   7 paid
4 started

4a 1 *started*   6 used
2 called   7 waited
3 finished   8 watched
4 posted   9 turned
5 noticed

Vocabulary common regular verb collocations

5 1 *g*   5 h
2 e   6 c
3 d   7 b
4 f   8 a

6 1 *moved house*
2 waited for a long time
3 prepared a meal
4 entered a competition
5 received an email
6 shouted at someone
7 posted a letter
8 visited a relative

6.3 Vocabulary development page 42

Vocabulary adverbs of degree

1 1 *There are a lot of very old buildings in the city.*
2 It's quite common to see tourists in my town.
3 The palace that we visited was really interesting.
4 The tour guide's talk was a bit boring.
5 The people in the hotel were very unfriendly.
6 The seats on the bus were a bit uncomfortable.
7 It's really cold here in winter.
8 It's quite expensive to have a holiday in England.

2 1 *a bit*   5 quite
2 quite   6 very
3 really   7 really
4 very   8 a bit

3a 1 He's a bit <u>unfriendly</u>.
2 Those <u>bags</u> are quite <u>cheap</u>.
3 She's <u>really</u> <u>friendly</u>.
4 This is a <u>very</u> <u>interesting</u> <u>article</u>.

Vocabulary review

4

in	last	ago
the sixteenth century	night	a long time
1974	week	three months
2011	year	two weeks
the summer		

5 1 *a competition*
2 house
3 a letter
4 a meal
5 an email
6 someone
7 a relative
8 a long time

6 1 It's very expensive. / It's really boring.
2 It's quite hot.
3 It's a bit cold.

6.4 Speaking and writing page 43

Speaking showing interest as a listener

1 1 bad news
2 interesting news
3 good news

2a 1 *bad news*
2 bad news
3 interesting news
4 good news
5 bad news
6 interesting news
7 bad news
8 good news
9 bad news

3a 1 *That's brilliant!*
2 That's great!
3 Really?
4 Poor you!
5 Oh no!
6 What a nightmare!
7 That's amazing!
8 That's awful!

Writing write a tweet or text message

4a 1 I want to go to Istanbul in April. Does anyone know a good hotel there?
2 I'm watching a great programme about famous singers. Is anyone else watching it?
3 I've just waited an hour for the bus! It was so boring!

4b 1 c
2 a
3 b
a Poor you! ~~Are you~~ home now? ~~Do you~~ want to meet for coffee later?
b Really?! ~~I~~ only watched 5 minutes. ~~It was~~ awful!
c Try Hotel Empress Zoe. ~~I~~ went there last year. ~~It's~~ really beautiful.

6.5 Listening for pleasure page 44

1 1 *writer*   4 town
2 plays   5 1616
3 films

2 1 *Shakespeare's birthplace*
2 Royal Shakespeare Theatre
3 the Grammar School
4 Bancroft Gardens
5 tourist information centre
6 Nash's House

4 1 *tourist information centre*
2 Shakespeare's birthplace
3 Nash's House
4 the Grammar School
5 Royal Shakespeare Theatre
6 Bancroft Gardens

103

Review: Units 5 and 6 page 45

Grammar

1.
   1. *'s buying*
   2. Could
   3. couldn't
   4. 's taking
   5. 'm working
   6. can
   7. don't usually pay
   8. is he cooking
   9. go
   10. don't like

2.
   1. *wasn't*
   2. weren't
   3. used
   4. were
   5. was
   6. walked
   7. looked
   8. chatted
   9. played
   10. Were

Vocabulary

3.
   1. *money*, sales
   2. really, blue
   3. shoes, return
   4. top, discount
   5. bit, gloves
   6. baker's, glasses

4.
   1. *house*
   2. wait for the bus
   3. a long time ago
   4. very nice
   5. hard
   6. dangerously
   7. post
   8. in

Speaking

5.
   1. *help*
   2. looking
   3. need
   4. try
   5. changing rooms

Unit 7 Health and fitness

7.1 My health, my business page 46

Vocabulary A healthy lifestyle

1a
   1. *sleep*
   2. do
   3. ride
   4. walk
   5. take
   6. eat
   7. do
   8. drink
   9. go

2
   a 7
   b 6
   c 3
   d 5
   e 4
   f 2
   g 1
   h 8
   i 9

3
   1. *eat lots of fruit and vegetables*
   2. drink eight glasses of water a day
   3. do an hour of exercise each day
   4. walk to work
   5. take the stairs, not the lift
   6. do physical jobs around the house
   7. sleep seven to eight hours a night

Grammar past simple irregular verbs

4a
   1. *rode*
   2. borrowed
   3. lived
   4. played
   5. paid
   6. stopped
   7. slept
   8. spent

4b
   1. *rode – irregular*
   2. borrowed - regular
   3. lived - regular
   4. played - regular
   5. paid - irregular
   6. stopped- regular
   7. slept - irregular
   8. spent - irregular

5

Verbs with regular past simple forms	Verbs with irregular past simple forms
believe – believed	*buy – bought*
change – changed	catch – caught
copy – copied	come – came
like – liked	drink –drank
look – looked	fly – flew
reduce – reduced	get – got
show – showed	hear – heard
study – studied	leave – left
tidy – tidied	put – put
use – used	sit – sat
want – wanted	take – took
watch – watched	write – wrote

6a
   1. *rode*
   2. put
   3. heard
   4. came
   5. flew
   6. caught

7
   1. *had*
   2. swam
   3. won
   4. left
   5. went
   6. drove
   7. ate
   8. told
   9. said
   10. thought
   11. found
   12. did
   13. ran
   14. felt
   15. did

7.2 Sporting heroes page 48

Vocabulary sports and fitness

1a

Verb	Go +	Play +	Do +
jog	fishing	basketball	athletics
cycle	to the gym	football	judo
run		tennis	yoga
ski			
swim			

2
   1. do athletics
   2. play football
   3. run
   4. go to the gym
   5. cycle
   6. jog
   7. play tennis
   8. do yoga

3
   1. *d*
   2. f
   3. e
   4. b
   5. a
   6. c

Grammar past simple negative

4
   1. *c*
   2. b
   3. b
   4. a
   5. c
   6. a
   7. c

5
   1. *They didn't go to Mexico.*
   2. We didn't stay in a hotel.
   3. The weather wasn't very good.
   4. He didn't win the competition.
   5. You weren't late for work.
   6. I didn't ski at the weekend.

6
   1. *bought, didn't buy*
   2. didn't go, went
   3. didn't do, did
   4. took, didn't take
   5. didn't lend, lent
   6. didn't start, started
   7. played, didn't play

7
   1. *started*
   2. didn't live
   3. ran
   4. wanted
   5. didn't think
   6. didn't agree
   7. didn't stop
   8. began
   9. entered
   10. didn't win
   11. didn't want
   12. decided
   13. started
   14. opened
   15. don't/didn't have

7.3 Vocabulary development page 50

Vocabulary easily confused words

1
   1. *a*
   2. b
   3. a
   4. b
   5. b
   6. b
   7. b
   8. a
   9. a
   10. a

2
   1. *told*
   2. went
   3. lent
   4. looked at
   5. took

ANSWER KEY

Vocabulary review

3
1 *walk*
2 take
3 ride
4 do
5 sleep
6 eat
7 drink
8 go
9 do

4
1 play
2 do
3 go
4 –

5
1 *have*
2 keep
3 learn
4 lose
5 meet
6 win

6
1 *take*
2 lend
3 go
4 watch
5 tell

7.4 Speaking and writing page 51

Speaking opinions, agreeing and disagreeing

1a a 1 *What's your opinion*
2 I don't know about that
3 Yes, but
4 I think
5 I agree

b 1 What do you think
2 I don't agree
3 for me
4 I don't know about that
5 That's right

2 1 *What do you think (of …)?*
What's your opinion (of …)?
2 For me, …
I think …
3 I agree (with that).
That's right.
4 I don't know about that.
Yes, but …

Writing post a website comment

3
1 *agree*
2 also
3 right
4 also
5 know
6 agree
7 true
8 too

Unit 8 Travel and transport

8.1 I went to … page 52

Vocabulary holidays

1a 1 *go on a tour*
2 visit an art gallery
3 meet local people
4 trek in the mountains
5 stay in a hotel
6 go swimming
7 go sightseeing
8 visit a museum

2 1 *stay in your own*
2 lie
3 went
4 another
5 with a group of friends
6 sightseeing
7 visited
8 stay
9 beach holidays
10 an apartment
11 around
12 got

Grammar past simple questions

3 1 *Did you go on your own?*
2 Did they visit the Natural History Museum?
3 Did she stay in an expensive hotel?
4 Did you take photos of the local people?
5 Did he buy a drink?
6 Did you have a guidebook?
7 Did I pass the French exam?

4 1 *Did you go on holiday last year?*
2 Did your parents have a good time in Budapest?
3 ✓
4 How long did you spend in Gambia?
5 ✓
6 Did they book the plane tickets online?
7 Whereabouts in Dubai did they stay?
8 Who did you go with?

5a 1 *When did you get back from your holiday?*
2 Did you have a good time in the USA?
3 Did John go with you?
4 what did you do?
5 How far did you drive?
6 did you stay in hotels?
7 what was your favourite place?

6a 1 they
2 he
3 you
4 I
5 we
6 she

8.2 Journeys page 54

Vocabulary transport

1
a 2
b 4
c 1
d 4
e 3
f 3
g 2
h 1

2 1 *a, b*
2 b, c
3 c
4 b
5 a, b, c
6 b
7 a, c
8 c
9 b
10 c

Grammar have to/don't have to/should/shouldn't

3a 1 *Passengers should follow the bus company rules.*
2 You have to buy a ticket from the bus driver.
3 You should offer your seat to an old person.
4 You don't have to book a seat.
5 You have to use the seat belts.
6 You shouldn't eat or drink inside the bus.

4 1 *Passengers should follow the bus company rules.*
You have to buy a ticket from the bus driver.
2 You shouldn't eat or drink inside the bus.
3 You should offer your seat to an old person.
You have to use the seat belts.
4 You don't have to book a seat.

5 1 *don't have to*
2 should
3 don't have to
4 should
5 shouldn't
6 don't have to
7 have to
8 shouldn't
9 should

6a 1 *should*
2 have to
3 should
4 shouldn't
5 have to
6 shouldn't
7 don't have to
8 don't have to
9 should

8.3 Vocabulary development page 56

Vocabulary expressions with *get*, *take* and *have*

1
1 ✗, ✓, ✓
2 ✓, ✗, ✓
3 ✓, ✓, ✗
4 ✗, ✓, ✓
5 ✓, ✗, ✓
6 ✓, ✓, ✗
7 ✗, ✓, ✓

2 1 *dinner*
2 a taxi
3 text messages
4 something to eat
5 a sleep
6 email

105

7 photos
8 long time
9 bus

Vocabulary review

3   1 *a beach holiday*, a city break, your own
    2 another country, your own country
    3 a group of friends, your family
    4 the countryside, your own country, another country

4   1 *lost*   7 local
    2 tour   8 rent
    3 sightseeing   9 stay
    4 sea   10 mountains
    5 lie   11 museums
    6 around

5

go by	go on	miss	take/get
bike	foot	*your bus*	*a taxi*
bus		your train	the bus
car		your plane	the under-
underground			ground
plane			the train
public transport			
taxi			
train			

6   1 *get a bus*, get a taxi, get a text message, get emails
    2 have a good time, have a shower, have a sleep, have dinner, have fun, have lunch
    3 *take a bus*, take a long time, take a shower, take a taxi, take photos

8.4 Speaking and writing page 57

Speaking at the train station

1a 1 *travel*   5 come back
    2 next   6 take
    3 cost   7 platform
    4 single   8 help

2a 1 *Hello. I want to get to Cape Town.*
    2 Tomorrow, if possible. When's the next train?
    3 OK, and how long does it take?
    4 Right. How much is a sleeper ticket?
    5 Just a single, please.
    6 600 rand ... OK. Which platform does the train leave from?
    7 Thank you.

Writing email: a perfect holiday

3   1 so   3 because
    2 because   4 so

4   1 c   3 b
    2 d   4 a

8.5 Reading for pleasure page 58

1   a marry   c silent
    b will   d quarrel

4   a Mary
    b Robert, John
    c Annie
    d Robert, Liversage
    e Mary
    f Annie

5a 1 c   2 b   3 a

Review: Units 7 and 8 page 59

Grammar

1   1 *I didn't go on holiday with my friends.*
    2 The train didn't leave at half past six.
    3 They didn't take a taxi to the airport.
    4 We didn't have an Indian meal last night.
    5 Sally didn't get lost in Berlin.
    6 You didn't send me an email yesterday.
    7 I didn't read this book last week.
    8 Sandro and Max didn't fly to Mumbai.

2   1 *did you decide*
    2 Did you buy
    3 did
    4 didn't have to
    5 did
    6 have to
    7 should
    8 shouldn't

Vocabulary

3   1 *tell*   6 jobs
    2 gym   7 bus
    3 yoga   8 foot
    4 jog   9 fruit
    5 borrow   10 drink

4   1 *have*   6 visit
    2 stay   7 take
    3 take   8 have
    4 go   9 meet
    5 go

Speaking

5   1 *your opinion*
    2 I think
    3 I don't know
    4 Yes, but
    5 I agree

Unit 9 Cooking and eating

9.1 Food and drink page 60

Vocabulary food and drink

1   1 *bread*
    2 jam
    3 honey
    4 yoghurt
    5 beef
    6 mushrooms
    7 rice
    8 lemonade
    9 salad
    10 olives
    11 pasta
    12 pears
    13 chicken
    14 sweetcorn
    15 noodles
    16 lemons

2   1 *olives*   7 pasta
    2 beef   8 yoghurt
    3 lemonade   9 jam
    4 sweetcorn   10 pears
    5 bread   11 mushrooms
    6 chicken   12 rice

Grammar countable and uncountable nouns

3   1 *U*   9 C
    2 C   10 C
    3 U   11 C
    4 C   12 U
    5 U   13 U
    6 U   14 C
    7 U   15 C
    8 U

4   1 –   8 –
    2 –   9 a
    3 –   10 a
    4 an   11 –
    5 a   12 –
    6 a   13 –
    7 a   14 a

5   1 *any*   5 any
    2 any   6 some
    3 some   7 any
    4 some   8 any

106

ANSWER KEY

6
1 *I'd like a sandwich, please.*
2 Are there any noodles?
3 We don't have any eggs.
4 They need some bottles of water.
5 Mark made some cakes yesterday.
6 Is there any pasta?
7 I didn't have any breakfast this morning.

7a
1 b 1, c 2, d 3, a 4
2 d 1, a 2, c 3, b 4

9.2 In the kitchen page 62

Grammar *much/many* and quantifiers

1
1 *How much time do you spend cooking?*
2 How much fruit do you eat?
3 How many eggs do you buy each week?
4 How much fruit juice do you drink?
5 How many times a week do you have takeaway food?
6 How many calories are there in a pizza?
7 How much salt do you put on your food?
8 How much milk is there in the fridge?

2
1 *none*
2 not much/not many
3 some
4 quite a lot of
5 a lot of

3
1 *a lot of*   4 a lot
2 None   5 Some
3 Not many   6 Not much, a lot of

4
1 *much*
2 some
3 quite a lot of them
4 a lot of
5 how many
6 not many
7 some
8 much
9 a lot of
10 None
11 much
12 some

Vocabulary in the kitchen

5
1 *c*   7 h
2 d   8 g
3 ✗   9 ✗
4 ✗   10 f
5 d   11 a
6 b

6
1 *b*   6 b
2 a   7 a
3 c   8 b
4 a   9 c
5 c

7
1 *roast jam*
2 chop rice
3 fry lemonade
4 bake yoghurt
5 mix food in a fork
6 boil butter

9.3 Vocabulary development page 64

Vocabulary say numbers

1a
1 *5,000,000*   5 3.9
2 ¾   6 18%
3 14th July   7 73°C
4 1967

2a
a *fifth*
b half
c seven thousand, four hundred and ninety-one kilometres
d two hundred million
e eighty-seven per cent
f two million, seven hundred thousand
g eighteen twenty-two
h the sixth of September
i twenty twelve/two thousand and twelve
j five point seven million
k thirty metres
l thirty degrees Celsius

Vocabulary review

3
1 *beef*
2 br<u>ea</u>d
3 ch<u>i</u>cken
4 hon<u>ey</u>
5 j<u>a</u>m
6 bottle of lemona<u>d</u>e
7 l<u>e</u>mons
8 m<u>u</u>shrooms
9 noodl<u>e</u>s
10 ol<u>i</u>ves
11 pas<u>t</u>a
12 p<u>e</u>ars
13 ri<u>c</u>e
14 sal<u>a</u>d
15 swe<u>e</u>tcorn
16 yogh<u>u</u>rt

4

Kitchen equipment and utensils	Cooking verbs
bowls	bake
food-processor	boil
fork	chop
frying pan	fry
kettle	mix
knife	roast
microwave	
oven	
plates	
saucepan	
spoon	

5
1 *the twelfth of May*
2 nine point seven
3 a fifth, a half, a quarter, a third
4 forty metres, six centimetres
5 billion, million, thousand
6 thirty-two per cent
7 minus ten degrees Celsius, nought/zero degrees

9.4 Speaking and writing page 65

Speaking in a restaurant

1
1 *Italian*
2 lunch
3 soup
4 pasta
5 a starter and a main course
6 two
7 water

2a
1 *Would you like*
2 Would you like
3 Could I
4 Could I
5 Could I
6 Would you like
7 Can I
8 And would you like
9 Can we

Writing asking about and recommending a place to eat

3a
1 *hope*
2 I'm looking
3 favourite
4 anywhere
5 a good place
6 need

3b
a 4   e 2
b 7   f 3
c 1   g 6
d 5

107

Unit 10 The world around us

10.1 The weather page 66

Vocabulary the weather

1.
   1 *foggy*, freezing, icy, snowy
   2 dry, sunny, warm
   3 cloudy, rainy, wet, windy

2.
   1 *rained*   4 shone
   2 blew   5 froze
   3 snowed

3.
   1 *ice*   5 winds
   2 snow   6 fog
   3 rain   7 clouds
   4 storm 8 sun

Grammar comparative adjectives

4.
   1 *lower*
   2 bigger
   3 earlier
   4 worse
   5 more interesting
   6 more expensive
   7 taller
   8 later
   9 drier
   10 fatter

5.
   1 *higher*   6 wetter
   2 colder   7 lower
   3 cooler   8 better
   4 hotter   9 more comfortable
   5 sunnier

6.
   1 *New York is older than Sydney.*
   2 ✓
   3 The weather is worse today than it was yesterday.
   4 My new job is more interesting than my old job.
   5 I think spring and autumn are nicer than summer or winter.
   6 Karachi is bigger than Islamabad.
   7 ✓

7a A weak sound, /ðən/.

10.2 Natural wonders page 68

Vocabulary nature and geography

1.
   1 *beach*   6 coast
   2 mountain   7 lake
   3 desert   8 island
   4 river   9 waterfall
   5 rainforest

2.
   1 *islands*   6 rainforest
   2 island   7 mountain
   3 coast   8 Lake
   4 Desert   9 River
   5 beach   10 waterfall

3.
   1 *north*
   2 north-east
   3 east
   4 south-east
   5 south
   6 south-west
   7 west
   8 north-west

Grammar superlatives

4.
   1 *largest*   6 driest
   2 busiest   7 most famous
   3 best   8 most popular
   4 easiest   9 biggest
   5 warmest   10 cheapest

5.
   1 *The Congo River is the deepest river in the world.*
   2 Summer is usually the hottest time of the year.
   3 What is the oldest city in the world?
   4 Is Mount Kilimanjaro the highest mountain in Africa?
   5 Which is the most interesting museum in Rome?
   6 That's the worst hotel in the town.
   7 Yesterday was the sunniest day of the week.

6.
   1 *the coldest*
   2 higher than
   3 the most beautiful
   4 the tallest
   5 worse
   6 the windiest

7a
   1 *the fastest*
   2 the oldest
   3 the most dangerous
   4 the dirtiest
   5 the hottest
   6 the best

10.3 Vocabulary development page 70

Vocabulary collocations

1.
   1 *score*   4 light
   2 high   5 bad
   3 heavy   6 mild

2.
   1 *a deep mountain*
   2 a mild storm
   3 a strong sleeper
   4 a hard coffee
   5 a close person
   6 high traffic

3.
   1 *winds*
   2 sleepers
   3 temperatures
   4 traffic
   5 coffee

Vocabulary review

4.
   1 *cloudy*, dry, foggy, freezing, icy, rainy, snowy, sunny, warm, wet, windy
   2 *cloud*, fog, ice, lightning, rain, snow, storm, sun, thunder, wind
   3 *to blow*, to freeze, to rain, to shine, to snow

5.
   1 *waterfall*   6 lake
   2 desert   7 river
   3 beach   8 coast
   4 mountain   9 island
   5 rainforest

6.
   1 *east*   3 south
   2 north   4 west

7.
   1 *storm*
   2 friend
   3 sleeper
   4 worker
   5 traffic
   6 prices
   7 sleeper
   8 weather
   9 accent
   10 coffee

10.4 Speaking and writing page 71

Speaking

1a
   1 *compass*
   2 cooking equipment
   3 first aid kit
   4 GPS
   5 lighter
   6 map
   7 sleeping bag
   8 stove
   9 tent
   10 torch

2.
   1 *I think we should take a torch.*
   2 I'd prefer to take a first aid kit instead of a stove.
   3 The most useful things to take are the sleeping bags.
   4 A map is more important than a lighter.
   5 Using a stove is a better idea than making a fire.

3a
   1 *it's dark at night*
   2 we can use wood to make a fire
   3 it's cold at night
   4 it's easy to get lost
   5 it's difficult to make a fire in the rain

Writing describe places

4 1 *b* 4 f
2 e 5 d
3 a 6 c

10.5 Listening for pleasure page 72

1a 1 recipes
2 ingredients
3 utensils

1b 1 R 5 I
2 U 6 I
3 R 7 R
4 U 8 R

2 1 *to boil* 4 garlic
2 to grill 5 olive oil
3 to wash 6 herbs

4a 1 *g* 5 b
2 c 6 d
3 f 7 a
4 e

5a 1 *down* 5 down
2 down 6 up
3 up 7 up
4 up

5b 1 up 2 down

Review: Units 9 and 10 page 63

Grammar

1 1 *some* 5 quite a lot
2 a 6 many
3 some 7 lemons
4 any 8 any

2 1 *highest*
2 most difficult
3 smaller
4 fittest
5 most expensive
6 cheaper
7 more dangerous
8 best
9 safer
10 worst

Vocabulary

3 1 a food-processor
2 a saucepan
3 a spoon
4 roast
5 chop

4 1 *island*
2 one point two million
3 a tenth
4 coast
5 mountain

6 hot
7 rain
8 high winds
9 mild weather
10 temperatures

Speaking

5 1 *the menu* 6 Can I
2 should 7 like
3 to order 8 prefer
4 have 9 instead
5 course

Unit 11 Working together

11.1 Community spirit page 74

Vocabulary verb + noun collocations (1)

1 1 give a present to someone
2 visit someone in hospital
3 teach someone to drive
4 help someone with their homework

2 1 look after a child
2 plant a tree
3 make some sandwiches
4 repair a bike
5 improve the town
6 paint the room
7 organize a party

3 1 *give* 6 make
2 improve 7 organize
3 help 8 teach
4 visit 9 repair
5 look after 10 plant

Grammar *going to* for plans and intentions

4 1 *'re going to organize*
2 are going to play
3 aren't going to sell
4 'm going to ask
5 aren't going to have
6 are going to make
7 is going to design
8 isn't going to help
9 'm not going to do

5 1 *What time is the party going to start?*
2 What are you going to wear for your interview?
3 Is Andy going to meet us at the airport?
4 What colour are we going to paint the bathroom?
5 Are your children going to go to university?
6 How is Alice going to travel to Nairobi?
7 Are you going to learn Arabic when you move to Bahrain?
8 Is Maria going to buy the cinema tickets online?

6 1 *What time is the party going to start?*
2 Are you going to learn Arabic when you move to Bahrain?
3 What colour are we going paint the bathroom?
4 How is Alice going to travel to Nairobi?
5 Are your children going to go to university?
6 Is Andy going to meet us at the airport?
7 Is Maria going to buy the cinema tickets online?
8 What are you going to wear for your interview?

7a A weak sound, /tə/.

8a We stress *not/aren't/isn't*.

11.2 Challenges page 76

Vocabulary technology

1a Across Down
1 *website* 2 smartphone
3 apps 5 text
4 GPS
6 tablets

2 1 *website*
2 smartphone
3 text
4 GPS
5 tablets

3a 1 *www dot nelson mandela dot org*
2 *anton at russorest dot com*
3 www dot bbc dot co dot uk forward slash news
4 joel underscore kubi at mailbox dot com
5 www dot white house dot gov forward slash
6 mark dash derby at mailbox dot au

Grammar infinitive of purpose

4 1 *to organize*
2 to sell
3 to teach
4 to show
5 to explain
6 to look
7 to find
8 to read

109

5   1 *f*   5 d
    2 c   6 a
    3 e   7 b
    4 h   8 g

6   1 *'re going to leave, to take*
    2 's going to get, to earn
    3 Are, going to buy, to wear
    4 are going to meet, to talk about
    5 'm going to ask, to lend
    6 's going to use, to write
    7 're going to make, to take

11.3 Vocabulary development
page 78

Vocabulary making adjectives stronger

1   1 *beautiful*, lovely
    2 brilliant, excellent, fantastic, wonderful
    3 awful, terrible
    4 freezing

2   1 *tiny*   4 great
    2 huge   5 crucial
    3 delighted

3   1 *Janine is a very nice person.*
    2 *His exam results were really brilliant.*
    3 Our neighbours are very unfriendly.
    4 Your dog is very noisy.
    5 The singer was really terrible.
    6 We made a really huge cake for John's birthday.
    7 The letter wasn't very important.

Vocabulary review

4   1 *help*   6 plant
    2 improve   7 repair
    3 look after   8 teach
    4 make   9 teach
    5 organize   10 visit

5   1 *A GPS*
    2 a smartphone
    3 An app
    4 websites
    5 A text
    6 A tablet

6   1 *at*
    2 underscore
    3 forward slash
    4 dot
    5 dash

11.4 Speaking and writing page 79

Speaking

1   1 *Shall I send him a text?*
    2 Why don't I give you a lift?
    3 I'll help you to look for them.
    4 Let me help you with it.
    5 Would you like me to show you?
    6 Shall I phone for a pizza?

2a 1 *Shall I send him a text?*
    2 I'll help you to look for it.
    3 Why don't I give you a lift?
    4 Would you like me to show you?
    5 Shall I phone for a pizza?
    6 Let me help you with it.

3a 1 *Shall I write that down?*
    2 Why don't I do that?
    3 Let me help you.
    4 Would you like me to print the posters?
    5 I'll email the design to you when it's ready.
    6 Shall I make a drink?

Writing a notice

4a 1 *I*   5 F
    2 F   6 I
    3 I   7 I
    4 F   8 F

4b 1 Wanted: chess players. Want to do something different at lunchtimes and make new friends? Join the office chess club. Come to Room 5 on Friday at 1 p.m.!
    2 Do you need a cheap room to rent for next year? Would you like to live close to the university with a friendly group of people? We are looking for a fourth person to share a student house. If you are interested, call Naomi Brandon on 08952 727445.

Unit 12 Culture and the arts

12.1 Artistic ability page 80

Grammar present perfect simple

1   1 *haven't been*
    2 hasn't stopped
    3 has sold
    4 's become
    5 's travelled
    6 have watched
    7 have built
    8 have sung
    9 hasn't recorded
   10 has made

2   1 *Have, heard, have*
    2 Has, recorded, hasn't
    3 Has, given, has
    4 Have, been, haven't
    5 Have, bought, have
    6 Have, visited, haven't

3   1 *We've visited Moscow and St Petersburg.*
    2 Have you read this book?
    3 We haven't had a holiday.
    4 All of the workers have gone home.
    5 Mandy hasn't found a job.
    6 Who has taken my bike?
    7 I haven't heard the weather forecast.
    8 He has washed the car.

4   1 a   2 a

Vocabulary verb and noun phrases

6   1 *a cinema*
    2 a play
    3 a dance lesson
    4 an instrument
    5 a painting lesson
    6 a classical music concert
    7 a film/movie
    8 a salsa class
    9 an art gallery

7   1 *Have*   6 see
    2 go   7 play
    3 Have   8 play
    4 go   9 see
    5 go

8a 1 *seen*, went   4 gone
    2 go, saw   5 had
    3 play   6 going, playing

12.2 At the movies page 82

Vocabulary films

1   1 *action films*
    2 romance films
    3 animations
    4 horror films
    5 comedies
    6 musicals
    7 dramas
    8 science fiction films

2   1 *action films*
    2 horror films
    3 science fiction films
    4 animations
    5 dramas
    6 comedies
    7 musicals
    8 romance films

ANSWER KEY

3
1. *favourite*
2. *set*
3. *about*
4. *it's*
5. *stars*

Grammar present perfect simple and past simple

4
1. *I've never had acting lessons.*
2. Have you ever walked out of a play before the end?
3. We've never been to a film festival.
4. Have you ever met a famous person?
5. Has anyone in your family ever been on TV?
6. Nadia has never sung in public before.
7. Have I ever forgotten to send you a birthday card?

5
1. *'ve, played, played*
2. *went, 've, been*
3. *read, Have, read*
4. *starred, has starred*
5. *Have, had, had*
6. *'ve seen, did, see*

6
1. ✗
2. ✓
3. ✓
4. ✗
5. ✗
6. ✗
7. ✓

7
1. *lasted*
2. *designed*
3. *made*
4. *was*
5. *have received*
6. *won*
7. *has had*
8. *has won*
9. *became*
10. *have ever refused*

12.3 Vocabulary development page 84

Vocabulary past participles

1

Regular past participles	Irregular past participles
act – acted	become – became
cry – cried	find – found
like – liked	have – had
play – played	lose – lost
stop – stopped	think – thought

2
1. *You've won the Oscar for best director.*
2. Who's drunk my coffee?
3. She's met someone online.
4. We've begun to work.
5. She's been/gone on holiday.
6. He's written a book.
7. I've given Tom some money.
8. We've been in the office all day.

3
Rule A: *won/won*, met/met
Rule B: *drunk/drank*, began, begun
Rule C: wrote/written, gave/given
Rule D went/been/gone, were/been

Vocabulary review

4
1. go
2. see
3. have
4. play

6
1. *been*
2. began
3. broken
4. drank
5. driven
6. ate
7. given
8. went
9. grown
10. heard
11. woken
12. won

12.4 Speaking and writing page 85

Speaking on the phone

1a
1. *it's*, Is
2. call me back
3. moment
4. Hang, just
5. Can, call
6. afraid, out of
7. have
8. Could I
9. take
10. on

2
1. I
2. F
3. I
4. I
5. I
6. F
7. F
8. F
9. F
10. I

3
a 7, 2, 4, *8*, 6, 3, 1, 5
b 3, 7, 5, 1, *8*, 4, 6, 2

Writing a review

4a
1. I was really excited about seeing the film, but the book was better.
2. My son doesn't usually like museums, but he thought the show was amazing.
3. I expected the film to be great, but it wasn't.
4. I thought the play was too long and the main actor was terrible.
5. They're playing again tonight, but I don't recommend going.
6. I enjoyed the concert, but the guitar player was a bit too loud.
7. I didn't expect the circus to be good, but it was amazing.
8. I thought it was fantastic and I recommend it to everyone.

4b
1. N
2. P
3. N
4. N
5. N
6. P/N
7. P
8. P

12.5 Reading for pleasure page 86

1
1. a bishop
2. a candlestick
3. a prison
4. a prisoner
5. a plate
6. a fire

3
1. *prison*
2. bishop's
3. open
4. kind
5. sister
6. afraid
7. dinner
8. candlesticks

Review: Units 11 and 12 page 87

Grammar

1
1. *They're going to organize a charity race.*
2. I'm saving money to buy a new bicycle.
3. He's never used a GPS before.
4. Is your mum going to teach you to drive?
5. We went to a concert last night.
6. Have you ever eaten Peruvian food?
7. We're going to go to the hospital to visit Kim.
8. You aren't going to have a lot of time tomorrow.

2
1. *are, going to do*
2. to buy
3. haven't had
4. are going to make
5. 're going to sell
6. bought
7. Has, made
8. borrowed
9. to see

Vocabulary

3
1. *after*
2. garden
3. make
4. plays
5. film
6. theatre

4
1. *been*
2. forgotten
3. a science fiction film
4. awful
5. freezing
6. really
7. tablet
8. app
9. Comedies

Speaking

5
1. *Shall*, for
2. Would
3. have
4. Could
5. back
6. don't
7. Hold/Hang
8. Let

111

OXFORD
UNIVERSITY PRESS

Great Clarendon Street, Oxford, OX2 6DP, United Kingdom

Oxford University Press is a department of the University of Oxford.
It furthers the University's objective of excellence in research, scholarship,
and education by publishing worldwide. Oxford is a registered trade
mark of Oxford University Press in the UK and in certain other countries

© Oxford University Press 2015

The moral rights of the author have been asserted

First published in 2015

2019 2018 2017 2016 2015
10 9 8 7 6 5 4 3 2 1

No unauthorized photocopying

All rights reserved. No part of this publication may be reproduced, stored
in a retrieval system, or transmitted, in any form or by any means, without
the prior permission in writing of Oxford University Press, or as expressly
permitted by law, by licence or under terms agreed with the appropriate
reprographics rights organization. Enquiries concerning reproduction outside
the scope of the above should be sent to the ELT Rights Department, Oxford
University Press, at the address above

You must not circulate this work in any other form and you must impose
this same condition on any acquirer

Links to third party websites are provided by Oxford in good faith and for
information only. Oxford disclaims any responsibility for the materials
contained in any third party website referenced in this work

ISBN: 978 0 19 456524 0

Printed in China

This book is printed on paper from certified and well-managed sources

ACKNOWLEDGEMENTS

The publisher would like to thank the following for their permission to reproduce photographs: Alamy pp.5 (plane/Wild Life Ranger, dancers/Hemis, games/Radarfoto), 16 (award, dance class/Stephen Power, Zumba class/James Davies, dictionary/Ben Molyneux Spanish collection), 20 (office), 21 (David Bagnall), 22 (7), 25 (Belchite/Pepbaix), 30 (painting/E & S Ginsberg, exhibition/AGF Srl, theatre/Len Holsborg, statue/AA World Travel Library), 32 (street/LOOK Die Bildagentur der Fotografen GmbH), 35 (Sanjay Borra), 48 (cooking lesson/Agencja Fotograficzna Caro), 52 (1/Agencja Fotograficzna Caro, 2/Alex Segre, 3/Paul Springett D, 8/Alex Segre, family holiday), 54 (train/Michael K Berman-Wald, car/Susan Norwood, cyclist/migstock, bus/Alvey & Towers Picture Library), 55 (card), 66 (Morocco/philipus), 69 (1/Mark Davidson, 2/The Art Archive, 6), 71 (6), 80 (dpa Picture Alliance), 81 (2/Blaine Harrington III, 3/Horizons WWP, 7/Mim Friday, 8/Oliver Knight), 83 (Tech Gadgets); Corbis pp.10, 13 (RV Atlantis/Dean Conger), 74 (man helping woman); Getty pp.6 (family), 13 (diver), 49 (Holde Schneider), 55 (card reader); Oxford University Press pp.4 (Hong Kong), 5 (pizza), 6 (fish and chips), 8 (dictionary, brush), 15, 16 (café), 22 (1, 2, 3, 5, 8, 9), 25 (giving directions), 30 (Factfile), 41 (man cooking), 44 (detail of cover of Oxford Bookworms: The Life and Times of William Shakespeare/Richard Allen), 48 (2, 4, 7, 8), 52 (5), 54 (tube train), 58 (all), 60 (1, 2, 4, 5, 7, 11), 61 (sandwich shop), 63, 66 (storm), 67 (New York), 68 (1–3), 69 (4), 71 (1), 72 (1), 74 (1), 76, 81 (6), 85, 86 (Les Miserables); Rex Features pp.38 (Hollandse Hoogte), 82 (Collateral Damage/Everett Collection, A Wedding Invitation/Everett Collection, The Simpsons Movie/20thC.Fox/Everett, Scream/Everett Collection, Ace Ventura/Everett Collection, The Sound of Music/Everett Collection, Gangs of New York/Everett Collection, The Fifth Element/Everett Collection); Shutterstock pp.5 (doctor, car, phones), 6 (shipping containers), 7, 8 (shelf, chocolates, pitch, bus), 9, 16 (jewellery-making), 20 (Ada, Darren, Elizabeth), 22 (4, 6), 27, 30 (man painting, 32 (mall), 36, 40, 41 (woman with boxes), 47 (both), 48 (1, 3, 5, 6), 52 (4, 6, 7), 54 (plane, taxi, pedestrians), 55 (train), 60 (3, 6, 8, 9, 10, 12–16), 61 (cakes), 62, 64, 66 (Iceland), 67 (map, Sydney), 68 (4–8, compass), 69 (3, 5), 71 (2–5, 7–10), 72 (2–6), 74 (2–4), 77, 81 (1, 4, 5, 9).

Illustrations by: Dylan Gibson pp.18, 28, 46, 86; Kerry Hyndman pp.24, 26, 29, 44; Joanna Kerr pp.11, 63; Gavin Reece/New Division p.34.

The authors and publisher are grateful to those who have given permission to reproduce the following extracts and adaptations of copyright material: p.86 Extract from Oxford Bookworms Library 1: *Les Misérables* retold by Jennifer Bassett © Oxford University Press 2012. Reproduced by permission. p.58 Extract from Oxford Bookworms Library 2: *Stories from the Five Towns* by Arnold Bennett, retold by Nick Bullard © Oxford University Press 2008. Reproduced by permission. p.30 Extract from Oxford Bookworms Library 1 Factfile: *New York* by John Escott © Oxford University Press 2008. Reproduced by permission.